To Beaut
my Beaut
daughters,
my granddaugh
With Love & Hugs.
Mom Gramma
A.K.A. Sherilp

CONVERSATIONS

with

DOG

Rennie Crossley

Tellwell Talent
www.tellwell.ca

ISBN
978-0-2288-2277-6 (Hardcover)
978-0-2288-2275-2 (Paperback)
978-0-2288-2276-9 (eBook)

Book Description

In a moment of time, came a special dog that would capture my heart and my soul. Her name is Zoey. I'm about to take her to Costa Rica. This would be the first time that I have ever taken a dog on one of my trips.

About a month before we left, I was busy in our garden courtyard doing garden things, when out of the blue, a voice spoke to me! It was deep, it was loving. It was the voice of God. He said, "Write your book through Zoey's eyes".

Well, I looked around and thought, OMG. What just happened? The last thing I was thinking of was writing a book. In the past I have often tried to write my memoir. Here lies the problem. I am a humorous story teller, it is the Ukranian in me! I make funny faces, constant hand motion, relishing in the telling. Yet, when I try to transfer this to paper, I could never find the flow, the Essence of Rennie. Over the years I tried and tried and finally gave up. Now God was telling me to write! Which tells me not only did He know my dilemma, He was clearly watching over me! My book is an attempt to share my journey through adversities and healings. Learning that when we choose the glass half full, we gain wisdom! So, it is with humbleness and humiliation that I share my memoir, as requested, with the Grace of God.

What a surprise when I next got on the computer and began to write through the eyes of Zoey. The flow was there, the humor was there, and thus began "Conversations With Dog".

Table of Contents

Dedications

This book is dedicated to Charlie, who showed me that I am a worthwhile soul. He taught me about love, forgiveness, and gratitude. One of his favorite advice, "Don't quit before the miracle happens." Thank you Charlie for the whispering gift you have bestowed upon me.

And to my sis Coffee, who puts up with my misguided humor and loves me anyways.

For Zoey, my furry best friend. You are the gift that keeps on giving, from life to the hereafter!

Thank you!

"Love is the Answer, what is the Question?"

John Lennon

"Always do right. This will gratify some people, And astonish the rest"

Mark Twain

"If you want God to laugh, Tell him your plans"

Woody Allen

1

Hello there, my name is Zoey. I am an adorable seven-pound, almost four-year-old female Shih Tzu. I was born August 31, 2003. My human master's name is Rennie and at fifty-six, she's pretty adorable herself. I call her my ma, even though she's not a dog. So, welcome to my life as a dog. Ma says I was one of thirteen pups, and she chose me, sight unseen upon hearing that I was the runt.

"Huh." I asked. "What is a runt?"

"A runt," Ma said, "means you were the smallest of the litter."

"Is that a good thing, Ma?"

"Oh yes," said Ma, "the best surprises come in little packages."

"Yay."

When my ma got me, I was so little, I fit in the palm of her hand. Within hours I had her wrapped around my little paw. I think since I was so little, she felt she had to protect me. I have to tell you that I took advantage of that.

One time I heard her call me a terrier, I was tickled pink. I hear that terriers are very cute till Ma informed me she did not call me a terrier but a terror.

"Ouch!"

Ma senses my hurt over this and along comes lesson number one. She said, "Do not worry about what people say about you, ever; words are just that, words." She said, "Think about what is being said and look for intention, and ask yourself, is it Ma's intention to hurt me? Chances are she is not, so quit the drama."

"Geez, I can see that life can get very complicated very quickly. So, call me terror, call me anything you want to, I am happy you are talking about me at all!"

Now as I look back, I can see how spoiled I was. Yet as a puppy, all I could think of was the fun of it all. Ma said she once heard this about puppies, that "when you watch them, you realize they believe they are the center of the universe and that the world is their oyster." *I ask, "What is an oyster?"*

And Ma said, "Oysters are bivalve mollusks that live on the seabed."

Huh?

Training for me was a little difficult. You see, the patio door to the outside was sooo big. When I sat in front of it, I was so little, no one could see me, so I peed right there on the spot. Wouldn't you? My ma knew we had a problem, and she put on her thinking cap (I never saw a hat on her) and got creative. She put some bells on a long ribbon and tied it to the door and when I wanted to go, all I had to do was ring those bells. I can tell you, I had as much fun ringing those bells as people had watching me ring those bells. Have you ever rang a bell and simply listened to it for the pure pleasure of it? I call it God's music, and I didn't even know who God was!

It wasn't long before I figured out that this lovely bell was also the answer to playing outside. Just ring those bells and out I could go and play, and I liked to play a lot. For two years, she said she felt like a yo-yo.

"What the heck is a yo-yo?"

Ma said, "A, yo-yo is a toy that goes up, down, for humans." *I did ask, didn't I? So, finally, she got rid of those bells, and I can tell you, I really miss them and wished I hadn't abused this privilege.*

2

I have a brother named Jazzie; he didn't seem to like me too much. When I first came home, he was forever smelling my bottom and then would run away. What's up with that? Ma said I will be doing the same thing to other dogs when I get older, something to do with dogs sniffing their way to acceptance. No, I will not be doing that, ever.

Jazzie is a black and white Lhasa Apso, and with those colors he looks like he is dressed in a tuxedo all the time. Ma especially likes to take Jazzie for walks around the neighborhood. She says he has a royal demeanor in his step and is a delight to follow. What does that mean? I believe I'm a princess, and she doesn't call me a royal-anything, except she once said I was a royal pain in her butt. Doesn't sound too royal to me.

In my opinion, Jazzie reminds me of a penguin, handsome in a penguin kind of way, know what I mean? But he sure is a spacey dog. Ma says he's socially challenged, whatever that means. He doesn't know how to react to people or other animals; he's plain weird. Ma says he's skittish on account of being abused as a puppy and now he is paranoid of others and noise, and cause of that, he has anxiety! "What is paranoid, Ma?"

" Paranoia is an abnormal tendency to suspect and mistrust others."

Told you he was abnormal. My ma's favorite story about Jazzie is his dislike of cars. Ma said he had this dislike from the day she got him as a puppy. As soon as he gets in a car, he starts to howl, I mean really howl. I have heard him and it isn't pretty. Ma asked her animal doc why he does that and the doc said he probably thinks he's going to his demise.

I asked, "What the heck is demise?"

"That means to die, then he'll go to doggie heaven."

"Is doggie heaven nice, Ma?"

"Oh yeah, imagine a heavenly oasis where there are fields and fields of grass and free food, and treats, and sun, and other dogs you love, and all you have to do is play as long as you like. It is pure joy and love.

I asked ma, "Why can't I go now. I want to go, who would not?" "Certainly you may go Zoey, just remember then you wouldn't be here with me, Jazzie, or Promise. As well you will not go on all the adventures we could enjoy. If I was sure that doggie heaven was what I wanted she could certainly arrange this." *Something about the way Ma says this gives me goose pimples, and I don't even know what a goose is. I think for now heaven can wait.*

Anyways, Ma says you can honestly hear Jazzie say my ma's name, Rennie, and it is really, really funny. Many folks driving with us have heard him and crack up laughing. When he isn't saying Rennie, he's howling. Ma says cars driving by probably hear him and must think she is abusing him, and she isn't impressed, but also cannot stop chuckling since he is sooo loud. Yet when Ma takes him to the beach, he knows that, and the howls become whimpers. Told you he was weird. This always amazes my ma. She says every dog she has had knows when she would turn down a certain street to the beach, and every one of them had reactional behavior, begin to go nuts, cry, scratch the window, howl. See, we do have some intelligence; we're not dumb mutts. It has to do with our senses, humans.

When I arrived, I found out Jazzie had a girlfriend named Hannah who was also a Shih Tzu and who had been sent to her demise four days before. Yikes, there's that word again, and now I was feeling sorry for Jazzie.

Ma has said there were some judgments about her getting another puppy so quickly. She says these judgments were unfair but knew that the judgments were not about her but about the people doing the judging. OK then. She explains that when it comes to humans and pets dying, "No one grieves the same and that there is no right way or wrong way to grieve. It is such a private experience for one and for all." She has also said we should never assume we know what another person feels or should feel, when they face death, and instead, be compassionate and of service if they need us. Also, that some humans even celebrate death; they believe that death is only a door to another experience of life and life goes on, like a chapter in a book. Once you finish one, you're on to the next.

"What is your belief, Ma?"

"My belief, Zoey, is when I die, I'm going home! My belief is so strong that I have no fear of dying. I kind of fear about 'how' I die, everything after that is pure joy. So, if I go before you, Zoey, celebrate me and know that I will be there for you when it is your turn, waiting at those Pearly Gates!" *"What's a pearly gate ma?"* "The Pearly Gates is the entrance into another universe created by God, surrounded by angels, and all your family and friends who have gone before you, there to welcome you. A lot of humans call this universe, Heaven."

" *Wow Ma, if I go first, I will wait for you by those Pearly Gates."*

"Thank you Zoey, I love you." *"And I love you Ma".*

Ma says each person has their own opinion on the interpretation of Heaven and the Pearly Gates. She says this opinion begins with their family's belief and whatever they teach you as a child, you repeat their belief. After all, these are your parents. If you cannot believe them then who can you believe. As we get older and discover other points of view, you begin to develop your own beliefs and then pass those on to the children you will have. It's wonderful.

3

*Back to Hannah's journey. Ma professes that I didn't replace
Hannah, that no one could, but that I was yet another gift
to share. Ma was grateful for the time she had with Hannah
and would never regret their time together. I like that. Ma
conveys she was with Hannah when she went to heaven, and
said the experience was very difficult and yet beautiful for
her.*

*Hannah had been Gramma's dog and Ma was with
Gramma when Hannah was purchased. Hanna was
purchased from a pet store and red flags were flying when
the salespeople mentioned a surgery Hanna would have to
have soon, but not to worry, the store would pay that bill. Ma
told Gramma maybe she should wait and go see some other
puppies but no, Gramma loved this little Shih Tzu so much,
she bought her in spite of the red flags.*

"What's a red flag got to do with buying a puppy?"

Ma said, "Red flags are warning signs, an instinct that
something is not quite right, and we should pay special
attention to them. When we do not, we are soon sorry."

Huh? Gramma did not pay attention to her instincts!

Unfortunately, Gramma had a lot of health concerns and when she went into the hospital for a month and Hannah was one year old, she asked my ma to take Hannah seeing that she knew she could not keep putting Hannah through all of this drama. Ma says that it's very important for dogs to have a routine and structure. Watch them in their environment and you can observe that they have their territories and boundaries and where they feel safe or not. Take dogs out of his or her routine and watch the change in their behaviors. I'm gonna watch out for this; I find it very intriguing.

Hannah's parting really hurt my gramma and she still mourns this dog. Ma says it was soon after she got her that she realized Hannah had allergies to the extreme. For six years, Ma did everything she could for Hannah but nothing worked. She even took her to the big city to what they call a doggie specialist and steroids were introduced. Now steroids are very complicated. They are a type of pain relief medication given pets for inflammation and allergies. It also controls allergy reactions, meant to be used for short term. Long term only in life threatening diseases. Hanna was on and off them for the entire six years.

Hanna and Jazzie went on many rice and chicken diets with no seasonings, cookies or treats. O' my animal god, how awful, I thought, and poor Jazzie suffered Hannah's allergies, too, cause they ate the same food. So, it was tough but Ma says Jazzie never ever complained, for his love for Hannah was sooo big. Hannah could do anything to Jazzie, and he looked at her with adoration.

Ma says, "Now that's unconditional love." *I asked her what that meant, I thought love is love.* "Oh no," *Ma said,* "love is vastly misinterpreted, and many people abuse the word love. Real love does not hurt and that real love has no expectations, the minute love hurts or we expect something, anything, it is not love anymore; it is some insecurity within ourselves." She also told me this, "No expectations, no disappointments." She says humans complicate the heck out of life and are always looking for something bigger or better or different than their life and that they will go to great lengths to find this. Ma says there is simply one question you could ask yourself for absolutely anything and get your answer immediately. That question is, What would love do? She asked, "Can you imagine what life would be like if all the leaders in the lands lived by this question?" What a world it would be!

Wow, could it be that simple? Ma said, "Yes." So, Ma had to create some serious experiments to feed Hannah. One time she bought raw buffalo from a specialty store, which is good for dog allergies, she heard. The meat smelled sooo wild that even the dogs were wary of it, and Ma says the fridge stunk like high heaven, which confuses me as one would think that "high heaven" would smell absolutely delicious. Evidently, not! Anyways, after about three hours in the fridge, she opened the fridge door and o' my goodness, the stink! She almost threw up. She had to throw out not only the meat but all the food, as the buffalo meat's rancid smell spoiled all that food. She took all the food to the woods by our house for hungry animals. Now, that's nice for a dog to hear. Hannah also had to go on these pills. The steroids began to take a toll on Hannah. So, finally Ma took Hannah to the animal doc for advice as Ma was becoming exhausted, never mind how Hannah must feel.

This animal doc had treated Hannah for a long time and suggested it was time to end Hannah's pain and to let her go. These kinds of decisions must take a toll on anyone having to go through this. Glad I don't have to make decisions like that. Ma says we are lucky to have people who make these decisions for us instead of living with severe pain. She says humans can't do that for other humans in North America, only animals. It is against the law in Canada, anyways. What? Yup, Ma says but the laws are slowly changing and it's about darned time.

Ma gets really upset at the injustice of this. She says the compassion we have with our animals is a beautiful thing. Yet, if we assist in helping a loved one go to their demise, we go to jail. We do live in strange times! Ma said, "Can you imagine what aliens from other worlds watching us say to each other?"

"Ma, what are aliens?"

"Aliens are beings in other planets in the universe.

They are not like us." She said she heard that earth is one of the youngest planets in the universe. And by judging our behaviors as human beings, she believes this.

Ma says, "I have a little sister Patti who lived in West Palm Beach at the time I went to visit a few years ago. She drove me everywhere, for errands and such. Here is what I noticed: it didn't matter who we met in a day, homeless people, store clerks, gas jockeys…she had something kind to say to everyone she met. Here's the shocker for me, and it is the reaction of every person she was kind to, they 'shined.' Seriously, I kid you not, their eyes just lit up, every one. It was such a lesson to me that I am grateful every time I think of her teaching me this kindness and not even knowing she was teaching me this kindness."

Ma tells me, "She believes that we are all connected, humans, animals, nature, trees, birds, the sky, and the stars." As a matter of fact, she says she read one day that the atoms we have in our body were atoms once forged in stars! Ma loves to remember this saying. It is so awesome and makes her feel that in the scheme of life, she matters!

"Wow, Ma, that's seriously the nicest thing I have ever heard. What is an atom?"

"An atom is the smallest particle of chemical element that can take part in chemical reaction." *Once again, I'm sorry I asked.*

So then ma knew the time had come to take Hannah to the animal doctor's to say good-bye. She was shaking. *I wonder what Hannah felt like?* Ma says the process went like this: "First they gave Hannah a needle to calm her down, like a valium." Whatever that is, but Ma says it's really, really nice. *I think we should all have some Valium,* and Ma says no, only some people need it cause they don't feel so *nice and the Valium helps them.*

"So how come when I'm having a bad day, I don't get any?" Humans, hard to figure. Anyways, then the doc gave her a cookie and Hannah began to gobble them up like crazy, so they kept giving her more and more, and the more they gave her the more she ate.

Ma said her response was, "Look at her, she's eating like there's no tomorrow. The day she took Hannah to the animal hospital, she was so torn. She knew she O' my God, there is no tomorrow." She didn't know whether to laugh or cry.

Remember, Hannah could never eat cookies cause of the allergies, and I think if I couldn't have cookies for years this would be a great way to leave as cookies are a dog's second-best friend. Ma says Hannah is eating lots of cookies now cause Ma believes she is now in the hereafter, and that in the hereafter, life is wonderful. I like that. She believes Hannah will be there to meet her when she goes to her hereafter. I don't know where the hereafter is, but I'm happy that there is one. I hope my ma isn't too excited to go yet. What would I do?

So, I plan to enliven this home and maybe they won't be so sad about Hannah. I run around chasing squirrels and yet spend hours lying in our courtyard watching ants work. They are amazing things! I never hurt them. I love them. I'm funny and adorable and play up to these attributes a lot. It's important for me to know I am as loving as Hannah. It's a lot to live up to, so no wonder I'm sooo tired at night. Ma says dogs live in the now, which is a gift from God, and that's why they call it the present! Ma says humans can learn a lot from animals about living in the now.

She loves Eckhart's Tolle's book called The Power of Now. She reads it a lot. She asked, "Have you ever seen an animal depressed about the past or fear for the future?" Good question. I can only speak for myself when I say the past is but yesterday's dream, and the future serves no purpose in the here and now. If that doesn't make sense, remember, I am a dog. One of Ma's favorite sayings she heard is, "If you have one foot on yesterday and another foot on tomorrow, you are peeing on today." Oh Ma!

Ma also read all the Conversations with God books and she studied the Course of Miracles book (a yearlong course) twice. *"So, what did you learn the most from all your studies, Ma?"*

Ma's answer was quick. "Forgiveness and acceptance." And Zoey the hardest person to forgive was myself

"Why, Ma?"

"Believe it or not, Zoey, I don't know that I have an answer for that. Maybe the answer is ahead of me on my journey. What I have learned is if you cannot love yourself, you cannot love another. When I learned this, I realized that the work ahead of me is to begin within. One of my homework tasks was to look in the mirror every day and say, I love you Rennie. I was amazed at how difficult that was for me. Although I kept it up day after day for a year. Somehow, it changed my perspective on myself. I was learning that I am a loveable person, that I could forgive my past wrongs and not hate myself. I have to give AA the credit it deserves here for their 12 steps that helped me achieve this healthier attitude. I could never have done this by myself."

"Wow, Ma, do you live every day like this?"

"Sad to say, Zoey, no, I don't, but it is a life lesson of mine and I am a better person today than I was a long time ago. These are all life lessons, and life lessons are never learned in one day. Understand, Zoey?"

"No, Ma, confused is what I am."

"No problem, Zoey, you are where you are supposed to be. Enjoy that."

4

We also have a silver Persian cat with the biggest golden-brown eyes. He doesn't even look like a cat; he looks like an owl. His name is Promise. What kind of a foolhardy name is that for a male cat? Ma states there's a long story to his name, but I am too tired to hear it. Maybe one day. Apparently, he almost became a star a few years ago for a Eukanuba cat food commercial, but at the last minute the shoot for BC was cancelled. Ma was terribly disappointed, but my gramma was here and when she heard this, she said, "Well, that's show business!" Everyone cracked up with laughter and gone was disappointment. I see now where my ma got her humor from!

Promise is bigger than both Jazzie and me. Yikes! But this cat is so laid back that you can't help but love him. Ma says when she takes the two dogs and Promise out to the pet stores or the mall at Christmas, no one pays any attention to the dogs cause Promise is the star. Everyone asked, "What is that?"

"It's a cat, for God's sake, what's so special about a cat?" Ma thinks she missed an opportunity for him to be in the movies. She says he's that adorable and eye catching. Enough *of the compliments for him, OK. More about Promise in a moment. Can't be good for a dog's ego, can it now?*

Also, the occasional frog visited our pond, and are they loud, my poor ears. When the first one came, Ma tells it like this: It was a mild misty spring evening and she had the patio doors open to our courtyard when she heard this weird noise (my ma knows all the noises around our house). She says all houses have personalities and their own language. Cool. Anyways, this noise got her attention and she could not figure out where it was coming from. She took a flashlight and went back and forth in the courtyard listening for this sound. Finally, she figured out it was coming from the pond. Sure enough, she spotted the frog and says it was sooo small, she didn't know such small things could make such big noises.

She says he burped till about one in the morning. Burped? Ma says a burp from a frog is their language and that's the name for their language. She says dogs bark, frogs burp. OK, I get it! A few days later, she ran into her neighbor, and he commented that he had heard that frog and mentioned it to a friend of his, saying my ma must have bought some frogs. And he wasn't too thrilled about this as froggy burps were heard around the neighborhood. Ha ha. The friend asked him if my ma had a pond and he said yes and was pleased that it was nature's gift, so Ma was off the hook.

"What does off the hook mean?"

"It means, Zoey, no one could blame me for this frog." *The frog came back a few nights later, then disappeared. I think Ma was happy and sad. She doesn't like to irritate the neighbors, yet she loves all kinds of animals, especially surprise visitors.*

Speaking of ponds, we also have, like, twenty-five fish. Who has so many fish? Ma explained to me that every spring, she waited for the fish to surface from winter hibernation and when they didn't, she thought they had died due to herons, raccoons, or bad weather. She would call them for days, then mourn for the fish, say a prayer for them in gratitude, and thank the animal gods for taking care of them.

She then restocked more fish for the summer, then miraculously, the winter fish appeared. She went through the same nonsense for three years yielding the twenty-five fish. She now has a net over the pond as she is assured that if the fish ain't floating, they are alive somewhere in that pond. They are pretty cute; my ma's favorites are the chabunkas. I think it is because it sounds Ukrainian and so is my ma. Psychologically, she is drawn to them. She tells me a story about when a carpenter was doing some work on our roof, and she was feeding fish, when she noticed something strange coming out of one fish's mouth and he was struggling. Ma thought he was choking and got really scared, so she ran and called the carpenter, telling him she had a crisis. Well, he got off his ladder so fast and followed Ma, thinking something was terribly wrong. He sees this fish that Ma was so worried about. She held the fish up and Rick the carpenter pulled out from its mouth an...ant. "Ain't that something?"

She was so thrilled Rick was there and helped save that fish' life. And Rick now has a fish story to tell. Ma gets tickled pink telling this story and laughs and laughs.

"OK, Ma, settle down."

5

Ma is very pleased that Promise the cat understands these fish are pets and not dinner. Promise spends hours watching them swim around without disturbing them cause as slow as Promise is (Ma says she gets that from her auntie Patti), he can catch mice, insects and never mind he got stung by a bee in his eye when he was little. That scared my ma. Back to the animal doc for fixing. Ma tells a story of when Promise was little, and they lived in a small town. She had him tied on a leash on her porch so he wouldn't run away, and a few minutes later she had this premonition, she calls it, and went out to see if the cat was OK; he was not. He had walked to the side of the house and dropped off the edge of the porch and was hanging by his neck, his tongue sticking out and everything.

Ma told Promise he had eight lives left.

I asked Ma, "What's a premonition?"

"We all have them, even animals, especially animals." She said, "Sometimes one feels a pang in their heart or stomach and knows instantly that something isn't right, regardless of the situation," and "when you act on this premonition it is a good thing, if you do not, bad things usually happen and you think, why didn't I listen to my premonition?" *I think I understand. I asked Ma if that's what Jazzie has when he gets into the car, a premonition that he's gonna die. Ma said,* "Well, yes, but that's a false premonition."

O' my animal gods, what confusion.

Last summer the weather was so nice, Ma left the patio doors open overnight and a neighborhood cat came a'visiting, right into our house, although Ma thought it was so cute. The next morning one of her foster kids, who loves Promise dearly, came to her room with Promise in his arms and said something was wrong with Promise. Ma took one look at Promise's eye and freaked; blood pouring out of his eye and she knew immediately that he had been attacked. So, once again, rush him to the animal hospital and amazingly he did not lose his eye, thank the animal gods. Ma found out the same day that the neighborhood cat she thought was so cute had gotten on the roof and had climbed into one of the kids' rooms window and thus the fight was on. The cat never came back and Ma wonders who got the best of who? So, she yet again had to make sure any windows without screens were closed. My ma really loves animals.

She thinks every species has a right to be on this earth, even rats, ants, and slugs. She told me a story about one morning last spring when she went into the kitchen and there were, like, twenty-five flies flying around. Her foster kids wanted to kill them, and Ma was horrified. Ma says she was in her Zen mood, whatever that means, and she got a glass and spent the day catching them individually and taking them outdoors, which is pretty time consuming and took her all day, but really nice for a dog to hear. Then the next morning she went into the kitchen and there were around fifty flies. Ha ha. Ma says she prayed to the animal gods, apologizing, and got out the Raid. Flies gone.

One day, a neighbor from across the street knocked on our door. It was Uncle Mike. He had his palm open and something was in it. He told my ma that one of his cats almost killed this beautiful hummingbird, and did she want to try to heal her? Ma took that dying hummingbird and thought this tiny beautiful creature surely cannot live through this. The poor girl was almost decapitated.

"What's decapitated?" I asked Ma.

"That's when someone slices your throat right through, and your head is cut off from the rest of your body." *Yet again, I am so sorry I asked. So, Ma got an aquarium from the garage and arranged a towel in it, put the hummingbird in and tried to give it water through an eye dropper. The hummingbird refused and lay there, not moving.*

Ma says she prayed to the animal gods and went into her medicine cupboard and checked on what she had that could help when she saw a container called Watkins Ointments. It was a Petro Carbo Salve. Huh? It said, "A pain-relieving ointment for temporary relief of pain and itching, sunburn, minor cuts, scrapes ...." Ma thought she had hit the jackpot. She got a Q-tip and applied this ointment around that hummingbird's neck and watched intently. After a few hours, that hummingbird suddenly began to flutter. Ma could not believe her eyes. She watched it for a while then took it out to her courtyard. She put the hummingbird on a picnic table beside a fence and a tree. After about fifteen minutes that bird flew up to the fence, then about fifteen minutes later, it flew to the tree, where it stayed for a long while. Ma was astonished; the thought that one could save a bird's neck with human ointment had to be a divine intervention, and she thanked the animal gods.

"What is divine intervention?" I asked.

"Divine intervention is when magic happens."

Huh? She will swear to you that in the act of saving this bird's life, this bird not only comes to visit but brings her entire family with her.

Ma declares, she thought it was such a touching story that she wrote to the Watkins people to tell them her story, and they did reply, thanking her for the story and nothing else. Ma was disappointed. She expected that they would somehow use it in a commercial, as it was a winning story for their product.

"Don't forget, no expectations, no disappointments, Ma." *I told her she should have put it on YouTube. Ha ha.*

6

As a puppy, I was pretty active. Sleep for fifteen minutes, play for one hour, twenty-four hours a day. Ma was very tired in the morning from being up all night with me. She says this is what it must be like to have a baby and wasn't too pleased with me since she really likes her sleep and is very grumpy if she doesn't get a proper night's rest. I happen to like the nights. Puppies can be very selfish, again believing that the world is their oyster! So, after three months of not sleeping, she finally took me to the animal doc and asked for doggie valium.

She asserts there is a lot of debate about pills. She believes pills can be a really big gift from God. She believes we as a people have come so far from the good old days, when people did not have the advantages of pills that we have today.

She says, for example, women going through menopause or others living through depression, anxiety, and the list goes on. She maintains if there had been anti-depressants or hormone treatments available back in the good old days that people would have been in church on Sundays and thanking their gods for these those days if they could have gotten hold of some Viagra, there would have been less farming, and more living and loving?

"What's Viagra?" I asked.

"It is one pill dogs don't have to ever worry about," *and I am yet again confused, yet oddly intrigued.*

She continues. Can pills be overused? Of course they can. Anything can be used and abused. One has to always have a balance whether it is with pills, alcohol, shopping or fine gifts that allowed them to improve their lives. And for men, don't you think in other things. Life is about balance and there the journey lies*!*

7

I asked Ma if she had depression when she was young. She said, "Well, Zoey, let me regale you with bits of my childhood. Lie down and put on your listening ears."

"What does regale mean?"

"It means to entertain with talk." *"Alright, Ma, regale me."*

I grew up on the wrong side of the tracks, one of the worst streets in a big city. I had an abusive father who was a very sick man. He controlled all of us. He was nine years older than my mom. My mom, 2 sisters, and I were all scared of him. Even though my mom was scared of him, had four girls with him. The times were much different back then. He was a pedophile, an alcoholic, a war veteran and he had rage, big rage. He beat my mom up a lot. She went to the hospital a lot as well. I remember him breaking a broom stick over my mom's back. As for us girls, his method of punishment was as follows. If we did something wrong, or angered him we had to kneel on the floor, facing the wall, with our hands up high. No bending of the elbows. He would then strap our backs over and over. We were only three, four, and five years old at this time.

That was the physical abuse. Then came the sexual abuse. My mom worked in a pub and she loved working there and had good friends. She worked evenings.

The problem was Dad was the babysitter. He would come to our bedroom where we all slept in one bed and he would choose one of us to go to their bedroom and sexually abuse us. It happened a lot. My youngest sister wasn't born yet. My sisters and I tried to put a dresser drawer against the door to stop him from opening the door. It never worked. I remember lying there and praying it wasn't me he chose yet feeling horrified that I was so selfish and crying for whomever he did choose.

When I was five years old, I finally told my mom and she was brave enough to call the police and have him arrested, even though she was scared of him. He was sentenced to jail for three months.

And my mom took him back! She sincerely believed he got help in jail. He did not. In those days, leaving your husband with four kids was not as easy as it is today. It wasn't long before the rage and the abuse returned, the violence escalated as did the sexual abuse. This went on for 2 more years.

Once again, there came a night when I once again told my mom that the abuse was still occurring. I told her this while she was at work. She told me to take the girls and go to our bedroom and she would have the police come as soon as she could. I did that, and for some reason my Dad had a feeling that something was up. He called a taxi and took me out of bed and had the taxi man drive to the hotel where my mom worked. He told the driver to speed it up and he would give him extra money. The taxi sped up and I was scared as scared can be. The good news was by the time we got to the hotel, my mom had left. He then had the taxi driver race back to our home. As we were pulling up to our house, there were police cars all around and he was arrested on the spot.

This time he was sentenced to two years in prison. Never to return.

8

This certainly fractured the family. My mom began drinking heavily and I became the mother to my sisters. I had to steal money from her purse to buy food for the girls. I called Children's Aid Society and they came to our home and took us all away. I was seven years old. Two of my sisters got to stay together for a while. I stayed in foster homes for seven years. And not one, many. My youngest sister lived in foster homes from the age of two to the age of sixteen.

To give you an idea what that was like, picture the first home I went to. Remember I said we came from the wrong side of the street; well, they found me a home on the "right" side of the street. Wow, it was a beautiful house and they had a little girl my age. I was seven. At bedtime, I shared a bedroom with her. She had this lovely four poster bed with lace all around it. It was like a princess room. I remember she asked her mom for a hot cup of milk before she going to sleep. And her mom brought it to her with love in her eyes. I have hated hot milk ever since. It was a frightening time for me; I was so out of my comfort zone, and what I felt most was shame. I felt I was dirtying their home with my very being. But being a seven-year-old, I didn't know what shame was. I was so sad, and lost.

The next morning the mother of the house woke me up with a very stern look on her face. She seemed angry. She told me to get dressed and to pack my bag, I was leaving. I was at a loss, no reason, just get out.

My social worker came and picked me up and took me to the big Children's Aid Society building. There, they told me that, unfortunately, I had lice in my hair and that scared the foster parents. Shame showed up again. In those days, this is how they handled lice. They cut your hair short, poured stinking stuff onto your scalp, put on a white net to hold it all together and you could not take this net off. This let everyone know, you were a dirty little girl with lice. I wanted to die, I was so very embarrassed, and my shame deepened. I heard much later that these good folks owned hair salons, and that's why they had such anxiety. Really?

I had some good homes, some not so good, but all in all, I felt a whole lot safer going to bed each night without worrying about abuse. And even in the loneliness I felt every day and night, at so young an age, I knew I was better off in foster homes. I often asked myself if being in foster care was worth it. It is difficult to explain to someone what going into a foster home is truly like.

Years later in a communication's class, the teacher wanted her class to write an essay on empathy. I remember it was a Friday, and somehow this subject irritated me. I went to a cabin at the lake for the weekend and said to myself, "You want empathy, I'll show you empathy," and wrote a poem called "Hear the Children." It is being used by some therapists and college communication courses teaching empathy! It isn't a happy go-lucky poem; sometimes the truth does hurt. And lots of people just don't want to hear a sad story. Somehow, it makes them feel guilty for having a far better life. Hey people, we all have adversity in life; it is what life is all about. We have it at different ages and stages. It isn't what happens to you in life, it's what you do with what happens to you in life. I was an active alcoholic when I wrote "Hear the Children," I was still in my victim role.

This poem explains how my childhood took me to a very dark place. The reason it was written wasn't to make one feel good, it was to make one hear.

Here's an example: when I was between five to seven years old, and all the abuse was going on at home, I didn't know what to do, so I got a bread knife out of the drawer, you know, the dull one, and I would pare the inside of my arm. This raised huge red welts. I did this over and over. Then I would go to school and make sure my sleeves were rolled up. I wanted someone to "hear" my pain by seeing the bruises. They saw, no one did or said anything. Hear it now, and feel my pain.

Hear the Children

Memories
Everlasting, ever cherished,
Childhood memories
With us forever.

Share with me
Thru a child's eyes,
Feel the emotions
We try to hide.

Understand my blues
As you never have before,
Walk in my shoes,
Come thru my door,

Let's begin with hunger
Can you feel the pain?
Your stomach no longer rumbles
It has nothing to gain.

Watch my brothers
Eyes round and wide,
Silently begging mister
But can you feel the pride?

Stare at my neighbor's
With their stomachs full,
Share the depression
Of a five-year-old.

Meet my mom
Don't you love her so?
But why does she drink?
As the violence grows.

Say hi to my dad
But keep your distance,
He's totally mad
And has no resistance.

Kneel with us
Our hands up high,
And scream with us
As his angry belt flies.

Can you feel the welts?
That never seem to leave,
A fear of belts
You are bound to conceive.

Can you touch the fear?
Share in the confusion,
Shed with us a tear
This is no illusion.

Watch my parent together
As they drink and play,
But like the weather
The storms not far away.

Cover your head
And hold on tight,
And pray they're not dead
Ain't this some fight?

Here come the men in blue
They've taken them both away,
Our home is no longer
Come follow the way.

Come take a ride
To a strangers home,
No place to hide
I am alone.

Feel the loss
But do not cry,
We gotta be tough
But don't ask me why.

The house so rich
The kids so straight,
Ain't life a bitch
Can you feel the hate?

Sit in my room
And feel the fear,
An ultimate doom
Why am I here?

Another move
Are you ready?
Get in the groove
Travellin's deadly.

And life goes on
Just don't forget,
I'm eight and growing
Are you tired yet?

The years pass by
New houses new friends,
And we no longer cry
We've learned to pretend.

Together again
A family reunion,
Yet somethings missing
Can you feel the confusion?

Do you feel lost?
We're all such strangers,
The past years cost
Those are the dangers.

And now we're grown
Independence begins,
On my own
Let's start with gins.

Drugs and booze
Can you feel the escape?
And on the move
Ain't life great?

Love and divorce
Don't count how many,
And we use the force
Yes, we learned plenty.

Avoidance is a game
Don't I play well?
No love no pain
I've been thru hell.

So, help build my wall
We'll keep people away,
And we'll build it tall
And alone we'll pray.

For all the sadness
A child knows
And we'll pray for empathy,
As this child grows.

Can you feel the weariness?
Are you tired too?
You can go home now
Goodbye and thank you.

As I recall these incidents years later, I find that sadness can still overwhelm me. Not just for me, but for all children of abuse. The good news here is with therapy, sobriety and a lot of work on myself, I don't stay in the sadness anymore. One of the powerful tools I learned about feelings is to honor them, the sadness, anger, or hurt. We all have these feelings and to push them down or run from them does us no favors in the long run. They just pile up, attracting more anxiety about them leading to all kinds of negative responses. Try giving permission for these feelings and allow fifteen minutes to an hour a day and no more, then to let it go! In time you recognize you need less time to hang on to the bad feelings. It is a remarkable process. How you handle them is the lesson. I no longer am the victim; I am the survivor! Years of different counselling worked it's magic. The one statement made by my counsellor was this: "If you are depressed about your father, he still has power over you!" Well, that got my attention. This helped me learned the gift of empowerment.

By the way. I got an A+ for this poem. Sherry, a school friend of mine, would get pissed at me as I put this poem in every essay final for the rest of my college courses and aced most of them. Ha ha. Always a silver lining.

Speaking of Sherry, she got to work in a group home for girls. Now I think I am funny, but Sherry is wicked with her sense of humor. One night she was getting dinner ready for her girls at the group home, and the girls were helping her. One girl was having a very bad day and at onc point took the bowl of salad and flung it at the wall. Sherry looked at the rest of the girls and, without missing a beat, said, "Guess we're having tossed salad tonight." I still crack up when she tells this story.

9

I went home when I was fifteen. My mom was sober now and had joined AA. She was doing so well yet having four teenage girls' home at one time was overwhelming and her sobriety did not last. A Children's Aid worker came to the home soon after and wanted to take us back to foster homes. I said, "No." We were not going to go through all that again. I told the worker that I would look after us till Mom got out of rehab. The good news was they put a worker in our home to act like a mother and we didn't have to go into any more homes.

I'm sad to say, we put this poor woman through hell. I hope they paid her well. I felt bad for my little sister who was then only eight. I convinced my mom to put her back in foster care because of her age and I believed she had a chance at normalcy in a foster home as opposed to our chaotic home. Mom agreed. I think now Patti would not agree with me. Sometimes choices are good and sometimes not so good. Look for intention, my intention was not to do harm, but to help. I often wonder if that was the right call to make.

I began drinking at a young age. Go figure! I loved it. Gone was the shame, the insecurity, the pain. I felt I was somebody. No victim here, I was all powerful! This went on for years. I loved people and parties. People ask why I drink. I would tell them, "Alcohol is my friend." Sad thing was I believed it. That's how much trust I had in mankind at the time. Took me a long time to learn alcohol was not the friend I thought it was. At eighteen, I was barred from parties. This hurt my feelings. One of the dysfunctional remnants of my childhood was rejection! Any kind of rejection. And evidently rage! I have experienced blackout periods in my journey of alcoholism. From my first drunk, till the day I quit. If I cannot remember my bad behavior, or rage because of black outs, how could I apologize to anyone? I truly didn't think I was an angry person. Time would prove otherwise. It is a bitch of a journey, my alcoholism.

10

I met my husband in a hydro camp up north near Gillam, Manitoba. Let's call him Mac. The camp was called Longspruce. I signed up for a job through some union and thought I was signed up as a hostess. Well, I thought, this would suit me perfectly! Working in a pub suited me to a T. Till I got up there and found out a hostess meant supervising about ten women for the lunch meal to about 1000 men. As scared as I was, I rose to the occasion, loving my job. And the men! They said if you couldn't find a husband in Longspruce, something was very wrong with you.

It was remarks like this that triggered my shame. I often felt no one could love a mess like me. In my early adulthood, guys would sing to me, "If you want to be happy for the rest of your life, don't get Rennie for your wife." I have laughed at that time and time again, except when I was home alone. It hurt; I didn't know how to feel better, so I drank more and became even angrier.

I saw the man one day who would become my husband. I picked him out from a line-up during lunch. He was so very handsome, looked like a happy Santa

Claus with his beard and red cheeks. I saw him again in the bar. Did I mention the bar in this camp? Huge! I saw him that night and I knew he was the one. We all went to the beach nearby where we had a bonfire every night. It was beautiful. When everyone was going back to their bunks, my new boyfriend asked if I would like to go for a walk. Of course! On the way back to our bunk houses was a small bridge, and Mac ever the gentleman offered to piggy back me over the water, which ended up with both of us falling into the water.

When I got to my bunk house, I woke everyone up, all the twenty women in my bunk house sleeping and told them to look at the guy I was going to marry!

In Longspruce, there were many proposals, especially from the bunch of Scotsmen. One night, approximately 500 Scotsmen were flown in to work in Longspruce straight from Scotland. What fun! Fascinating. That right or left turn we take at critical moments which define our journeys.

I wrote a poem for Longspruce to best describe my time there. Going to share it with you here.

"Long Spruce Epitaph"

Monday calls for relaxation
Relieving past intoxication,
Ahead me shines the telly lights
Blessed are those Monday nights.

Tuesday believes in limited action
Drinking reduced to a tiny fraction,

Recuperation, still a fight
Thank heaven for movies on Tuesday nights.

Wednesday promises one night out
With the boys there is no doubt,
Come see, come saw, what can I say
Confusing is a Wednesday.

Thursday holds uncertainty
Not ever knowing where I'll be,
Whatever party to come my way
Unreliable is a Thursday.

Friday expects another drunk
In the pub or in the bunk,
Knowing feeling higher than kites
Difficult are those Friday nights.

Saturday knows a celebration
Tomorrow's day off, a real occasion,
Drink all eve and what a sight
Nasty is a Saturday night.

Sunday morn, o' lord is me
Pass the bottle, I can barely see,
Body and nerves shot to a frazzle
Damn these Sundays are such a hassle.

My favorite memory of Longspruce was with a
bunch of us on the beach were drinking and talking
when suddenly the sky began to give us a light show! It

was mesmerizing. I cannot even find words to describe what was happening. I had never heard the words aurora borealis, known as the northern lights. I call it God's light show. The peak time to see them will be 2024. This happens every eleven years. And the further up north you are, the better the show. The best places to capture the true beauty of God's light show in Alaska, The Yukon, and Ireland. The sky danced for us, all these brilliant colors flying by. It was coined aurora borealis by Galileo Galilei in 1619. Aurora means morning light coming from the south. Borealis means morning light coming from the north. I googled this info for you!

You never saw a bunch of drunks lie so quietly. It was certainly a spiritual experience. It lasted for hours. I wish I could convey in better words the joy of it all. If you ever get a chance, put this one on your bucket list. I promise you, you will never regret it.

I followed Mac to Vancouver after Longspruce. We lived together for three years and then we got married. The marriage lasted six years.

Mac was a journeyman carpenter, and an excellent one at that. We had to chase jobs at times and travelled throughout Canada. One of my favorite places we experienced was Rankin Inlet, Nunavut (Our Land) an island in the North West Territories. It was located on the west coast of the Hudson's Bay, 300 miles north of Churchill. He was contracted to build houses for government workers. He had been there awhile when he suggested I join him. Hey, I'm in! I had a toy dog, a bishon frise named Kiwi. We flew in one day in August, it was a balmy 44 degrees fahrenheit. Their hottest day is in

July at 66 degrees. The Inuit people are delightful. Do not call them Eskimos as I did. This is insulting to them. As we landed, I was waiting for the airport to release my dog from the luggage area. I waited and waited. No Kiwi. Apparently they lost him in Churchill, forgot to put him on the place to Rankin Inlet and would return him the next day.

Mac was there to meet me and off we went to my new home in Rankin Inlet, by three-wheeler. Cars were a rarity as was roads. Rankin is a very barren land. I counted one tree, no leaves. One could see for miles.

Now picture my new home. It was the garage of Mac's boss. It had no insulation, no indoor walls, nor carpets, no anything. A bed, a dresser and a roommate shared our home. A sheet separated us. Privacy, what privacy? Lovely! It was dinner time and Mac took me to the big house to see what we could eat. He opened the fridge and there staring at me and yes, I do mean staring, was a half-plucked duck. End of my appetite.

There was a big store called "The Bay". Most items could be found there. Food was very expensive in Rankin. They also sold beer. Problem was you could only buy one 12 pack case a week. And you had to sign for them so they knew you had your limit.

I was so hungry so I went to the Bay and I bought a package of six pork chops. Here's my big idea! I would go to a friend I had met on the plane, who had an apartment and cook up these chops with wonderful seasonings and I took them back to my hacienda and hid them on a shelf in my garage thinking when I got really hungry I could just go and get me a pork chop! As I was thinking how wonderful they smelled I decided I should at least eat one as they were warm. I went to my hiding place and no pork chops! Fool that I am, forgot to think of animal senses. They were faster than I and I was so disillusioned. And hungry. The dogs won. I lost. Again.

One day Mac got the experience of a lifetime. He got to go on a whale hunt with some Inuit men and he was so excited. Now in those days, there were no cel phones, pagers etc. Yet, the women of Rankin knew exactly when the men were returning and the female community went down to the beach to watch their men come in and sure enough, here they came. With a whale!

Well, the men dragged that whale onto the beach and the women had their "oolo" knives (rounded like a half moon) and sliced that whale from one end to the other end. Out came the intestines, and the party was on! The women brought the intestines to their homes and set them to boil, as the party rolled on. Tonight was a feast. This was day five for me.

The next evening, I took Kiwi for a walk to a little store five minutes from our hacienda to pick up some milk. On the way, there came a sound behind me of a three-wheeler racing by. As I looked I saw that he was an older man and held a rifle and yup, he shot my dog, just like that. I was stunned. I went running back to the bosses house crying, thinking my darling dog had died. The boss had Kiwi on the kitchen table and within seconds, he took out his oolo knife, cut open the bullet wound on Kiwi and sucked out the bullet. Wrapped up the wound, no need for a vet. Cause there were no vets!. Done!

Yes, I flew home the next day with Kiwi. First place I took him to was a vet and surprisingly, the vet stated Mac's boss did a fine job removing the bullet. Lord o Lord. I still am delighted to have experienced the Inuit way of life. I will always have fond memories of them. There is a saying, Muk Tuk Kanupik ehhh! I think it means "hello friend".

11

Our wedding night was typical for the drama surrounding our relationship and alcoholism. After the dinner and dancing, we were given a room as a gift in the same hotel, for our wedding night, which was very nice of the hotel, as we were leaving the following day for our honeymoon. The problem arose when this nice hotel also gave my maid of honor a room for the night! Right next door to us!

The party was on! Mac and I were having fun in our room, when in his tipsy behavior, he fell off the bed. We were laughing so hard when there was an awful pounding on our door, from next door. It was one of my friends who had heard him fall and believed he was beating me up. She was yelling, "I know he is hurting her," and trying to rush in to rescue me. Mac was not an abusive man. I told Mac to relax and let me handle this. I went to the party room and what a party they were having! I told them all to leave and decided to clean up the room a little as it was a mess. When I was done, I went to go into our room and the door was locked. I knocked and knocked and no answer. I went to the other door and knocked and knocked and no answer.

I was so embarrassed. I guessed he had passed out and was not going to answer the door! I didn't know what to do, so I ran. Out the hotel doors into a taxi, no money, no shoes, crying, telling that taxi driver (who was a woman) that this was my wedding night and woe is me! She drove me home and was so kind, she did not even charge me. I spent the night with my dog Kiwi. When Mac got up the next day, he called the office to ask, "Where's my wife?" I am sure that if we had never lived together, I would have been mortified. Strangely enough, for me, it was life as usual.

Our honeymoon was about a lot of alcohol, drama and nonsense. The day we got home, my mom told us we had to go see her immediately. I knew something was wrong. As tired as we were, we went over to her home. She then informed us that my father, who was not invited to the wedding, committed suicide the morning of my wedding! She didn't want to tell me the day of the wedding so as not to spoil the day. I appreciated that. All I can say about this news is if he was going to go out this way, I wish he had done it a lot sooner and have fewer victims. I had not forgiven him yet.

The most gratitude I had for Mac was that he ever wanted to marry me in the first place. "Remember the refrain from my younger days? If you want to be happy for the rest of your life?" Married life was dysfunctional as you can imagine with a pair of alcoholics. We should have ended our marriage after one year, never mind six years.

One year, near the end of our marriage, Mac came home all excited. "Rennie, there is a contest on the radio for McDonald's. They are bringing out a new product called McRib. They said to send in a jingle, and you could win a trip to Jamaica. This is perfect for you." Mac was always supportive with my writing and thought I could win. At the time I became excited too. After I wrote one jingle, I read it to my boss at work. He read it and suggested I do something more original. I felt defeated. When I got home, I told Mac what he said, and I threw it away. Mac read it and loved it and took it out of the garbage and sent it in. I wrote another jingle and sent that in. Well, months later, I got a phone call from a radio station stating I had won second place in the McRib contest, winning a one-week trip to Jamaica! I was sooo excited. I asked them, "Which jingle won?" Believe it or not, it was the one I had thrown away. I still remember that crazy jingle. It went like this:

> Ronald McDonald had some ribs, E I E I O
> And tickle my tummy these ribs did, E I E I O
> With a McRib here, and a McRib there
> Here a rib, there a rib
> McRibs everywhere,
> Ronald McDonald thanks a might,
> For another McDelight!

At this time, I had to go down to the radio station for publicity photos and such. I saw a huge mail bag, filled with jingles. I asked, "Could I rifle through them and read some?"

They said, "Sure." Well, I laughed and laughed. There were funny ones, stupid ones, political ones and they all were terrific. I often wonder how judges pick out winners.

Glad they picked mine! Jamaica was a hoot. I really was happy to share this trip with Mac. He had paid for so many in the past.

Not long after this trip I learned that my younger sister was missing. She is one year younger than me and has two young boys. She was addicted to pharmaceuticals. Mac and I were not getting along. I called him at a friend's and told him my sis was missing and his response was cold. At that moment, I felt so alone, as I never have before, even when I lived in foster homes.

The day before she went missing she had spent a night in the hospital, an overdose. She was found on a street unconscious. She left the hospital in her hospital gown and no one saw her since. Me, my Mom and my sisters went looking for her everywhere they could think of. I had a Himalayan cat named Cali. On one morning Mac went off to work and Cali and I were just lying in bed when out of the blue this cat simply jumped out of my bed right into the window! She fell back on the bed and was fine. I was not. I took it as a sign. I called my Mom, and as we were talking, I could hear someone was knocking at her door. I hung up and raced to her home which was around the corner from my home and sure enough there were the police. They had found my sister. She had been found in an empty apartment lying under a kitchen table that was there and yes, she was deceased. They called it a suicide. We knew better. The police knew better, but did not have enough evidence to charge anyone. At this time I believed if my sister was not an addict and maybe if we were an important wealthy people, we would have had a proper investigation into her death. For some strange reason, I once again was ashamed that we were poor. I had survived a lot of deaths up to this point, yet the death of my sister really sent me into a deep depression that lasted about a year.

It was this tragedy that made me realize my relationship was reaching its end. I don't think there is a worse feeling of feeling alone in the middle of a relationship.

One day soon after this trip, Mac and I had yet another argument. He went to bed saying he wished he had never married me, how he hates me and hates Canada. This is an old rant. I have heard it over and over. Alcohol was always behind the statements.

Something happened to me this time after hearing this. I woke up the next morning and told Mac it's over. We are getting a divorce. He went to work as usual and while he was gone, I found him a nice apt. When he came home from work, asking as usual, "what's for dinner honey?" I gave him the apt. address and suggested he get going on this. He was shocked. And angry. He left the same day. Interesting enough, I believed that if Mac ever left me, I would be devastated, that my life would be over. Instead, I felt this huge weight off my shoulders. And I never looked back.

12

When my youngest sister called me one day, she said she had joined AA, I was shocked. I didn't think she had a drinking problem and if she did, I now knew I had to get out of denial and look at my drinking. In the back of my mind, I knew I was an alcoholic, but if I admitted it, then I would have to stop and change, which was frightening for me. Alcohol was part of my entire life; how could I live without it? I remember a friend once commented on her sobriety; she said what she missed the most was having a glass of wine at dinner. I laughed. I missed having a bottle of wine at dinner. Supposedly, every alcoholic reaches their own bottom. Here was mine.

I was at a bar one night and I got into an argument with a black woman about being black (I am white). I insisted to this woman that I knew what it was like to be black and the woman realized she was dealing with a nut and tried to get away from me. I, of course, was having none of that; I had to win the argument and, eventually, the woman left the bar. But I wasn't finished. Somehow, I had gotten this woman's phone number and called her at home. After one call, the woman refused to answer.

What I now believe I was trying to get across to this beautiful black woman was that I knew what it is like to be a minority. In my drunken stupor, I missed the boat on being the messenger. Ha ha. If I have the opportunity to ever see or hear from her, I would so apologize to her.

This rejection was playing deep in my mind and heart. I see now that shame was a part of my suicide ideology. The thing is, I didn't know it at the time. All I knew was I was hurting. A victim once again. This time I was going to do it right.

I have tried to commit suicide a lot in the past. One such day, I was feeling suicidal and called a therapist I had seen years before. I said to the therapist, "I'm feeling suicidal," and the therapist's response was "Aren't you always?" I laughed so much; it took away my depression that day.

This day was different. There was no one I wanted to call. It was morning now and I ordered some sleeping pills from the pharmacy and had to wait for hours before they were delivered. In the meantime, I was drinking, and I spent the day writing goodbye letters. By the time the pills came, I was ready. I took the whole bottle of pills.

When I woke up the next day, I looked around and knew, this wasn't heaven! This attempt sent my depression into total grief. I had, in fact, reached my bottom. I did something I had never done before. I began to talk with God and instead of apologizing yet again, this time I asked him, "Why do you want me alive?" This was an unusual question, and somehow in this question, divine intervention occurred. Most of my life I would ask myself why people wanted to live. I truly could not understand

and believed the smiles and laughs and happiness I saw from people were fake. And I was so unhappy that death clearly seemed a finer place than here. Not once did I think I had anything good to offer society, and my self-esteem, well, what self-esteem? This question was a novel concept for me.

13

I needed help and called an AA hotline. The next day, I attended my first AA meeting. Today, I have over twenty-eight years of sobriety. And not one attempt at suicide in my sobriety! At this date, my younger sister has thirty years sobriety, my other sister has twenty-seven years sobriety and my mom has forty-nine years sober. Good Lord, pretty good for a family of alcoholics!

When I first went into counselling after two years of sobriety, my counsellor asked me, "Why are you here?"

"I want to know why people want to live. I do not."

Good start! She counselled me for two years. I also took a course revealing your inner child. I have to tell you that this three-month course was my toughest counselling to go through. I wanted to quit every time I went.

At one point, the counsellor asked us all to lie down for a meditation session. (There were about eight of us.) The counsellor put on some nice music and began, "Close your eyes and take your child to her safe place." When I heard this, I instantly recognized my child did "not" have a safe place! I realized in that second that as a child I never had a safe place, and I didn't know what to do. I was lying there making crazy faces and beginning to cry. Bless this counsellor who picked up on this immediately and she came and whispered in my ear, "Take your child to your safe place today." Brilliant! My whole body relaxed, and I was able to breathe and know that today I have a safe place. Whew, that one was tough.

14

After about a year with my counselor, We were wrapping up an hour long session, not concentrating on anything heavy at the time, when out of the blue this beautiful deep voice spoke gently in my ear. He said, "Get off your knees!" WHAAAT? My counselor noticed a change in my demeanor and asked me what was wrong. I told her, and here is how she interpreted this for me.

I was having difficulty with religion. A lot of people in AA say if you want to get better and you want help, get on your knees and pray. I would try that, but I hated doing this and always became more agitated than peaceful. My counselor, bless her heart, had been paying attention to my story. She said, "Rennie, when you were little and received punishment from your dad, it came in the form of kneeling and having your back strapped. Then in your Catholic faith, you had to kneel when in confession, apologizing for your sins. In both cases you were reprimanded by males. An apology was always required from you. The message you were receiving every time you got on your knees was you are a very bad girl and you must be punished." Wow, I have to tell you, the healing from this announcement was simply huge. I was to learn in this part of my journey that the word "shame" was the feeling that had ruled me throughout my life. The moment that became clear, I ran to the bookstore and got every book I could on shame to heal and heal I did.

One of the gifts God's word taught me is that I don't have to be on my knees to pray. My God is open to my conversation and prayer, anywhere, anytime. It all made immediate sense and saved me an extra ten years in therapy! Talk about being in the right place to have received this gift! Although it should not surprise me, considering the source! I was learning a lot about who I am and why. More important to me was the biggest gift God gave me was his acknowledgement of me, me, little Rennie! Remembering this never fails to put a smile on my face or bring tears of joy to my very soul. I am worthy, he tells me. I am loved. I forget that too often. I often heard this beautiful saying, "If you could see, what God sees in you, you would smile a lot" Thank You, God.

From then on, in AA meetings, when I would hear anyone talking about getting on their knees, I would be right behind them saying, "Not necessary, get off your knees." Think about this, especially for women. Girls, ladies, what does being on your knees conjure? Exactly!

My doc at the time says she believed that I was probably depressed for years prior to drinking, considering my childhood. She put me on Zoloft, an anti-depressant. The best way for me to describe what these anti-depressants did for me was this: Imagine being so very sad, knowing you had lots of tools in your soul to heal, but the sadness was so huge, you could not reach those tools. After about six weeks of taking them, I felt like I had come home to myself. As crazy as this sounds, I think only others who take anti-depressants get this. No, I did not space out or get high. Some folks believe anti-depressants are feel-good pills. Sad to say. Now when I get emotional for whatever reason, I am able to go to my tools and deal with the issues with clarity! Instead of my depression lasting three weeks to a month, now I can let depression go after three hours! It was with this clarity I realized how screwed up I truly was.

The important thing AA taught me is, even in sobriety, life does not change. What changes is my perception of life and how I react to life. This poem changed me from the inside out.

In AA, they have the St. Frances Prayer, and it became my long-term goal. After reading this prayer, I realized that my whole life had been lived backwards! I say this with a grin. Totally backwards. I chose to seek comfort, forgiveness and love. I knew that there was not one line in this poem that I followed in life. Quite the challenge. It will take me a lifetime to get on track, yet it is a goal I try to live one day at a time.

St. Francis Prayer

Lord, make me a channel of thy peace –
that where there is hatred, I may bring love –
that where there is wrong, I may bring the spirit of forgiveness –
that where there is discord, I may bring harmony –
that where there is error, I may bring truth –

that where there is doubt, I may bring faith –
that where there is despair, I may bring hope –
that where there are shadows, I may bring light –
that where there is sadness, I may bring joy.

Lord, grant that I may seek to comfort, rather than being comforted –

to understand than to be understood –
to love than to be loved.
For it is by self -forgetting that one finds –
it is by forgiving, that one is forgiven –
it is by dying that one awakens to Eternal Life.
Amen

"OK, Zoey, sorry for taking up your time. You are a very good listener and may I remind you that I took you to lots of AA meetings, and what did most people say, *'Que Linda'.*" Ha ha. Only in English, it was "how sweet." *I have to say as a dog with an ego with mine, I preferred Que Linda!*

"You would quietly sit in my lap, and you know at AA meetings there is a lot of clapping going on. Always in celebration of a point of view or someone celebrating an AA birthday that deserved a clap. And every time they clapped, Zoey, you would begin to bark." Well, the AA folks loved it. As did I.

15

Ma called her animal doc to talk about what to do about my nighttime play and the sleep she was losing. The doc sent her to a pet behavioralist who informed my ma that I was in control of her and ma had none. It's called "being the alpha dog!" Ha ha. I am the alpha dog! Yet, I instantly knew this was not going to be good news for me. Ma laughs, saying she was shocked to see the simplicity of this. So instead of pills, I now sleep in a kennel by mom's bed, which is OK, but I'd rather be with her on her comfortable mattress. I sooo take advantage and don't seem to learn that there are consequences for my behavior and some consequences suck. Ma explained the need to look at the positives. Now I had my own safe place to go if I ever needed some space, and no one else was allowed in my space…Hey, I like that. She doesn't even remind me that she, not I, is now the alpha dog!

Ma is a single foster parent and has been fostering teenagers for over thirty-one years. She has homed over 250 teenagers. Ma says cause she was a foster kid, she had an invisible bond with the kids she takes in, a real empathy she says. "What's empathy?" I asked. She reminded me that empathy is when you authentically identify with a child or their issues. She asked me if I remembered "Hear the Children" and if not, did she want me to read it again?

"O' no ma, I remember, no reason to read it again!" Sheesh, fast thinking on my part!

She tells kids coming in that "We are all foster kids." Seems to work for the most part. She understands teens well, says it is the toughest ages that humans go through, what with changes in hormones, feeling powerless, not a child anymore yet not an adult either, questioning everything as well as chemical changes in the brain. Ma says one tip for parents is to try to empower teens whenever you can. They are experiencing feeling powerless and they don't even know it. All they know is something has changed, and they are not happy campers. Her tip is choices! She says it is so important to offer choices whenever you can as this also makes them feel empowered and it works. She says, parents, even if you have to consequence your kid, give them a choice of two consequences and watch the kid engage. She believes the biggest choice teens make is with peers. Ma says it doesn't matter what walk of life they come from, their choice of peers in their teens is a critical choice and if they choose peers in trouble, well, trouble follows them.

It's important to remember that the biggest gift we give our kids is independence. We want them to fall while we have their backs. They learn by mistakes, not successes or safety.

16

Having had the privilege of fostering kids anywhere in Canada, I chose to move around. For the first ten years, I fostered in a big city. I like to say, big city, big problems. Some of the biggest issues that came my way included gang violence, prostitution, guys introducing our fragile girls into prostitution, which was hard to overcome. These guys made these girls feel special, told the girls they loved them, bought them clothes, gave them money, alcohol, introduced them to drugs and all of a sudden, they had to pay the piper and prostitution was forced. Usually by then, they were hooked on drugs. And all those gifts stopped. And the love turned to abuse. Bullying was another big deal in big cities, and we didn't even have the internet yet!

One of the plusses of living in a big city is the wonderful choices of restaurants. With four boys who were disadvantaged in life, I decided that once a month, I would take them all to a restaurant of a different culture. Now, here is what happened: the boys loved it! They would dress up, which in itself was a marvel, and they would be on their absolute best behavior. Lots of hands-on learning during these moments. This never failed to put a smile on my face. They always tried their very best and were literally gentlemen. These are the gifts I get from fostering!

Through the years of fostering, I also got the amazing opportunity to foster teens from around the world. This was very cool. I have had kids from Afghanistan, Turkey, Ethiopia, Trinidad, Kenya, the Philippines, China, and Portugal. Probably more than I can remember. I get them to teach each of us about their country, which gets pretty amusing. All the kids seem interested and are very vocal in sharing their own stories. More gifts for Rennie.

Bullying affects a teen's self-esteem. I remember one boy I had who was not the most popular kid, being a little backwards and shy. One day his social worker and I were talking to him about his behavior at school, which was increasingly getting worse. He looked at us and through tears, "How do you think I feel when kids don't even talk behind my back, they tell me to my face how ugly I am, how stupid I am, they spit in my face?" As he is crying, my heart went out to him. How do you answer that boy in that time? Is it enough to say, "Hey kid, this isn't about you, it's about those bullies." Or, "You will be fine. You are a wonderful boy." These lines just don't work. This boy went through hell, day after day. Wished they had a Dr. Phil at the time. He didn't stay long in my home. I often think of him and send a prayer his way.

At another time I had four boys in my home. One boy who was shy and quiet as well, became a victim of bullying right in my home. When I found this out, I had a serious conversation with the boys stating that this home is a soft place to fall, that this home is a place where everyone is safe. I warned them about zero tolerance on bullying and warned them if it continued, I would show them the door. They seemed to listen and acted apologetically.

I found out about a month later when this abused boy left my home that he was no longer a victim of bullying, but when they were at the bus-stop the boys made him lick their shoes. Paranoia was always felt. In my home and out of my home. Kids sneaking kids in the house, drinking, drugging, running away from home constantly. I did room searches almost daily in the city. When I would find drugs of any kind or drug paraphernalia, I would drop them off to the local police station and leave a note to the boy who owned the drugs, that they could now pick up their drugs and paraphernalia at the police station. Not one kid ever commented or asked where his or her stuff was. God bless humor!

One of my frustrations as a foster parent was the Young Offenders Act. As an example, because I went into their rooms for searches and confiscated whatever was illegal, the police could not charge them as it was an invasion of their privacy. Really! Yes! I really believe kids today are not held accountable enough for their bad criminal behavior.

Speaking of room searches, one day I was doing my regular search when in one bedroom I heard a very strange noise coming from the closet. I was scared to go in there but go in I did. And what did I find? A chinchilla! What? I have to say it was the cutest thing. I had never seen one till that day, although I had heard of them. They look like big rats with beautiful fur. I took him out of the closet and made a room for him in a large aquarium that I had in the garage.

When the kid came home, he saw the chinchilla and knew he was busted. The kid said, "Please, Rennie, can I keep him?" I do not allow kids pets anymore. Learned my lesson. Teens are not very responsible looking after themselves never mind their pets. I asked him where he got it from, and he said a friend of his had it and the friend's parents wouldn't allow him to keep it, so he gave it to my boy. For some reason, I relented. I allowed him to keep it and would monitor his progress in looking after it. Maybe this could teach him something good. It was so cute! The kid was thrilled.

When I went to bed that night, I realized something wasn't making sense here. I had a hunch I was told a lie. This story didn't make sense. And then I had an idea. The next morning, I called the local pet shop and I asked, "Do you have a missing chinchilla?" They replied, "No, we don't, but our sister pet shop in the south had one stolen the other day." I laughed, letting them know, I have the chinchilla and would be returning it that day, and did. The boy couldn't say much, now could he? Whenever I found drug paraphernalia I would drop it off at the police station and when the kid came home I would tell him or her that I found it and they could gladly pick it up at the local police station! It was hard not to laugh. They certainly didn't find the humor in it. Yet what could they say?

A boy who was in his introduction meeting in my home actually said to me and in front of his social worker, "Nice house, lots to steal." I invested in alarms for inside, never mind outside, the next day.

There was one boy who had lived with me awhile. Nice kid. He had just gotten off the phone and was crying. "What's wrong?" I asked.

"My mom won't buy me a gun."

I looked at him. "That's so sad, I'm so sorry. Why do you need a gun?" I was being facetious!

"The kids at the mall hate me and want to jump me."

"Really, I said, for this reason you think a gun is the answer? Do you not think that the solution lies in "Staying Away From The Mall!" A couple of boys were listening in, so it was time for a home meeting. We began to talk about guns until I realized this was crazy. I told the boys I don't ever want to hear about guns in this home, nor any other weapons. There are so many stories. I find them fascinating.

Then I got to move to a small town. Small town, small problems. What a beautiful town! I was fostering two kids here. It was like day and night. I call town kids city wannabes. Kids were polite, kind, went to school, didn't throw things, and did lots of community activities. It was like another world. I realized little towns remind of a saying I have heard all my life and that is that it takes a village to raise a child. There seemed to be much more inclusiveness in towns as opposed to cities. One could get lost so much easier in a city compared to a town.

I lived there for two and a half years and as beautiful as it was, I missed diversity. And against my intuition, entered into a two-year contract with four beds in another big city. Again, big city, big problems. Here is my favorite story from this time.

One night I was asleep when I heard this very loud bang. This bang was right next to my bedroom, which was my bathroom. I had four teen girls asleep and my job now was to protect them. I cannot believe how scared I was. I tried to dial 911 on my phone and found I could not stop shaking and the phone fell and then went dead. I knew instantly that the phone wires had been cut. I ran to my purse to grab a cell phone to dial 911. God Bless these folks.

It was 6:00 AM, and they kept me on the phone as they dispatched officers to my home. About five minutes later, the 911 operator told me to go downstairs to the back door as the officers had arrived. I was so darned happy. I opened the door and there were four of them, all laughing. Why? I was so confused. They told me to follow them, and at the back of my house was a very long patio, in the middle of the patio were soffits, mangled, and lying all across the floor. The perpetrators were in the roof, probably laughing too. They being racoons. Yup, a whole family holed up there, partying till they ripped off the soffits! That was the noise. I burst out laughing now too. And no, not one girl woke up!

It was said, back in the day, a person would rather their home be robbed by drug addicts than teenagers. It was explained that drug addicts came to your home and knew exactly what they wanted, and in and out and gone. Teenagers, especially if there was more than one, had egos to protect. It's called the "gang mentality". They have to prove to their peers how tough they are. And teenagers live in the moment, not realizing the consequences ahead of them. They act irrationally and cannot be trusted to do more than just rob your house. And the damage they could do, all for a laugh. And not to be outdone, one would up the ante and do even more damage. Many sad stories.

17

With Ma's experiences as a foster child, she thinks she understands foster kids at a deeper level than one who has never lived in foster homes. One year, in celebration of Mother's Day, she was invited to be on TV honoring foster mothers. She was on a panel with three foster moms. The host asked questions to each of them. Questions about fostering. And throughout the hour, folks could phone in and ask questions themselves or comment on something said. Towards the end of the show, one person called in to say that if she had to be in a foster home, she'd pick my ma! Yay Ma! I thought. Ma was tickled pink, says it did her ego good!

She credits Oprah for some dream Ops had one day (Ops is Ma's nickname for Oprah). Ops was flying with her guru and as they were flying over a vast field of children, Ops said to her guru, "What can I teach those children?" and the guru answered, "It is not what you can teach the children, it is what can the children teach you." Ma says she got goosebumps at the profoundness of this statement. There's that word again, and I still don't see any goose!

She said she never looked at a kid the same again. She said when kids challenge her, she asks herself what she is meant to learn. This takes the negative out of the situation and becomes creative instead. It has worked for her for many kids, and she is so grateful to Ops.

All kids come with baggage, as do adults, by the way. The good and bad. Ma says it like this: these kids are conditioned by their life, their family, their culture, their school, their peers, and others. Ma has to figure out what issues are negative for these kids and how to help them turn them around. First, you have to remove their conditions, then recondition them, which takes years, and Ma realizes time is not on her side, so she can only start the journey of this process. They take what they learn from her and expand on it or not.

Ma makes sure she says at least one profound thing to each kid, each day. She thought that when they are older, they will remember this and pray it helps. Till one day one of her kids came back, now about twenty-five years old and she said to Ma, "When you said a certain thing, it changed my life!" And it was never the profound thing Ma remembers saying! She cracks up laughing and learned that she needed to be careful with every word said to kids, as you have no idea what they are taking with them!

Ma says dogs have the ability to feel authentic spirits, and they also can feel immediately who to shy away from. Ma says that is an awesome gift she wished humans had. Ma talks about a time when a few of her boys got together and put one of her older dogs, Mugs Malone, in the microwave oven. They hadn't turned it on, thank the animal gods, and Ma didn't hear about it till after the boy had left, and she was so upset. Can you imagine how upset ol' Mugs felt? She now has the dogs sleep in her room every night.

Most kids won't let Promise the cat sleep in their room cause he snores loudly, drools something horrible and is always wanting to go out. He also sheds hair like crazy. Kids quickly learn to not let him in. Ma says she prays a lot for Promise cause she can't be around him all the time. There have been a few who haven't mind that crazy cat, and Ma is tickled pink when she sees this. She talks about one boy who loves Promise a lot. One morning she heard voices, panicked and peeked into the living room at about 6 A.M., only to discover that this boy was on the couch having a conversation with the cat. You can call that sweet, I call that nuts! Ma says she is always amazed at the healing process animals lend to her home. Some of her kids have been so damaged that trust with people is very limited, and it's a long way to bond with them, but when they come in and are welcomed by the cat and dogs with kisses wagging tails, smiles come quickly. I am happy that the sight of me cheers a child. This is what Ops calls giving, and I have no problem giving kisses. Ma also says that she never demeans these kids with name calling. What she tells her kids who give her a hard time is this: "I love you, but your behavior leaves a lot to be desired." She strongly believes that when these kids hear this, they are not damaged further or lose self-esteem. The one thing Ma is careful about is never, never, shaming a kid.

I asked her if she had any funny stories about her kids. Ma said this one is one of her favorites.

She had a boy; she will call him Nick. Nick was an identical twin and his twin's name was Tom. It was April first and Nick was lying in his room when his phone rang, and soon after, he came into the living room looking nervous and upset. He told Ma he had to go down to the police station cause the police believed he robbed a house the night before. The police told him there were witnesses and it was important for him to turn himself in right away. Nick was understandably upset, and Ma knew this couldn't be true as Nick was home all evening with her. Ma quickly remembered that this day was April Fool's Day". It also was one of her mother's favorite days, and she knew right there it was her mother playing a trick on poor Nick.

Ma let Nick in on the gag and she and Nick decided they would give her mother some payback.

By now, his twin brother Tom arrived to help my Ma move to another house. Ma and Nick told Tom what her mother had done to poor Nick. They then shared with Tom the gag they were about to play on Ma's mother.

They had to stop at her mother's place to store some boxes in her mother's garage, and the boys came with her. A block away she dropped off Nick to walk slowly to her mothers place while bringing Tom, the twin in with her to her mother's. (Now, Ma's mother did not know that Nick had a twin brother). Her mother opened the door and immediately began teasing the boy she thought was Nick, laughing and hugging him, mussing up his hair, saying"I sure got you, didn't I?

"O' yes," said Tom playing the game.

Then the door bell rang. They both went with her mother to answer the door and when it opened, there was Nick! The look on ma's mother's face was priceless. She kept looking at Nick, at Tom, back to Nick, back to Tom and the boys were having a hoot.

Nick said to Ma's mother "Now, who got who?" Ha ha.

18

"Travel Zoey, is so important to me. When I was young, two of my biggest escapes was books and church. My first trip outside of Canada, was to Barbados in the Caribbean. I was young, twenty-three, and living the life. I had been invited there by a friend I had made in Longspruce. Her family lived in Barbados and I was delighted to have this opportunity. I sent a letter stating my arrival day.

As I was getting off the plane, the very smell of Barbados filled my lungs, the heat was filled with aromas I had only read in books. The warmth of this country embraced my very being. I was in heaven. It was like having my previous books come to life. I was hooked.

Since then, I knew travelling would become a big part of my life. It seems to me I tend to love the heat, the hotter, the better. Loved big ol' fans, not air conditioning. Loved running around barefoot, always. Simply loved the outdoors.

Upon arriving in Barbados, the airlines had lost my luggage. No problem they said. Call us tomorrow and it will be here. OK then. In the arrival section, I searched and searched for my friend and time flew by and I was alone. No one came. Now here is my dilemma. I didn't have her address. All I remembered was her name and that she came from a village called "Fitz Village". I had no idea why no one was there and was beginning to get a little scared. I didn't have a Plan B. A taxi driver noticed my discomfort and asked what was wrong. I told him. He began to laugh. He stated that Barbados was a very small country, everyone knew everyone. He made a phone call, drove me to Fitz Village right to the address of my friend! He stated everyone knows of the girl who lived in Canada and was home for a visit. No one was home and that taxi driver told me to just enjoy the home, door was unlocked, so I just walked in and waited. Everyone was at a wedding and they would be home soon. They were, and my friend was shocked to see me there. The letter I sent her arrived a week after I arrived! Her family was amazing. They were so very kind and to this day I have fond memories. When they showed me by bedroom that night, I got ready for bed and went to fold down the blanket and there covering my entire sheet was "ants". O'my, I thought that this is so not good… I let the mother know, she stated, "no problem" took the sheet outside, shook it out and remade my bed. It was a very itchy night for me.

I learned quickly to adapt and not freak out. When in Rome!!!

My dearest story from Barbados was on New Year's Eve. I was invited to the president's New Year's Eve celebration. Wow. Folks from all over. It was fascinating. An English lord walked towards me. He walked with a cane, and he looked like a typical old lord; he had a long scrunched up face, and there was an arrogance he tried to portray. He shook my hand, his palm was fishy, soft, and creepy. While he was doing this he placed a small piece of paper in the palm of my hand all folded up. I was so excited to see what it was. Well, imagine my surprise when I saw it was his hotel name and room number. I was not amused till I thought about it and humor once again kicked in. What a story to share with my friends. And no, I did not ever see him again.

The South Pacific quickly became one of my top places to visit. One of my favorite places was Fiji. When I travel, I like to get in right with the folks of whatever country I am in. I don't like being a tourist; I want to experience the true people, not the tourist areas. I hung out with the restaurant staff in Fiji; they know where the real fun is. They took me to a hotel one day and in the vestibule was this large fountain in the middle. The thing is, it wasn't only water in this fountain; it contained a coffee-like substance called *cava*. Anyone can go and have a sip of this *cava*. As I was told, *cava* holds an ingredient like cocaine and when you sip it, it numbs your mouth. I don't remember getting very high from it; it just felt fun to have my mouth numb, for some very strange reason. I was thrilled to go back to my tourist friends and share this experience with them. The tourists we met never heard such a thing. What fun.

I remember a time when I went to Acapulco. I met a bouncer on the beach, He was from Acapulco and we became friends. One night, he asked if I would like to meet his family. I said of course, I was actually honored. And we walked and walked. It was a beautiful night. Once we were out of the tourist area, it became so much darker, no lights. And paths instead of roads, and when we got to his place, I was astounded. There was a house, but it had no walls. It had a roof, pillars to hold the roof up, furniture, totally exposed to the outside. Chickens running around, dogs barking, even a few pigs thrown in. I loved it. It brought me to a sense of humbleness to have shared this experience. No one had to worry about theft. I mean, how easy would it be to just walk in and take whatever you want? Trust held in these villages was just a given. It seemed an important message for me.

I lived in a city in Mexico called Merida, north of Cancun for six months. What fun. The plan was for me and my friend Yumi to live in Mexico for a year. Yumi, one of my very best friends who showed me how to have fun without alcohol. We would sit at outside restaurants on the Paseo Montejo and just watch the people, meet people, drink lots of coffee and laugh. We laughed so much. I adored my friend Yumi. She ended up going home after three months, her first grandchild was on it's way. I missed her dearly and my first stop was the liquor store! I went home after six months. I realized that not working and nothing much to do with my days, life became super boring. I missed home. I missed my dogs, my kids, so home I went. I was surprised how paranoid I was, for months after returning to Canada. It seemed to me that Mexico was way laid back compared to Canada. No yelling, little fighting. Hardly any swearing. Merida was a place I returned to time after time for years. I have many friends there.

I loved New Zealand and Australia too. For two countries that are so close, I was surprised at the differences. New Zealand is like a small replica of the Kootenays, BC. I learned to fly fish in New Zealand. And yes I was the only one to catch a fish, there was four of us. There are no straight roads in New Zealand. Curves everywhere. Gorgeous country. Perth, Australia was flat like the prairies. Different aura between New Zealand and Australia. Fascinating. Going to the zoo to see kangaroos and koala bears was a must.! I could have stayed there forever.

19

Sept. 11, 2001 changed travel forever. The experience of watching a plane fly into a tower was stunning; watching two towers collapse was unbelievable. This day reminds us around the world how hate can touch us all. The magnitude of the horror still haunts me, never mind the folks of New York, the mothers, fathers, wives, and husbands, firemen and policemen who perished that day. Heartbreaking does not begin to describe that day. I now knew what horror felt like. Once again, I felt so helpless. This problem around the world just seemed so, so big. How the heck could I begin to be of help?

Prayer. That is the only way I could be of any service to the victims, and to the world. Stop the fighting. Stop the hate. Stop the judgment.

I wrote a poem.

"There Is a Solution"

Muslims and Christians, to name a few
Every religion, has paid its dues

What one and all, seem not to know
Membership is free, we reap what we sow

There is a solution, you won't want to hear
It doesn't involve weapons, nor chemical gear
Innocents won't cower, for death will cease
There is a promise, for global peace

With war there comes, a terrible fate
You can delay the terror, but never the hate
Your solution is temporary, it never lasts
The time has come, put war in the past

Israel's and Palestine's, to name a few
The time for love, is long overdue
Hug your brother, and sister kind
Love is the solution, in prayer you'll find

For we are one, in all the land
We cannot fix, what we don't understand
This solution so simple, if we all do our part
Listen to your neighbor, and bless his heart

Hinduism and Judaism, to name a few
In the name of Religion, let's start anew
The solution is love, it opens the door,
For peace and love, from shore to shore.

20

Two years ago, Ma went on holidays to Cost Rica. When she got home, I was so excited to see her. Golly, I had missed her. I began shaking like a nut. My tail was going bonker, waggin away. I kept jumping on her. Couldn't leave her side cause now I was thinking when is she gonna go and leave me again? I must stay close.

The energy in the house when she leaves almost hurts. All I can do is eat and sleep and wait. She was so excited about her trip that she wouldn't shut up about it. Something about loving the monkeys.

"What the heck is a monkey?"

"A monkey *is the cutest animals that are the closest specimen to man."*

Huh? And then Ma decided she may want to live in Costa Rica and she booked another month-long trip, and guess what, she was taking me! Yahoo!

When Ma gets ready for a trip, she lays down her suitcase in her bedroom for days before leaving and slowly packs. As soon as I see that suitcase, I now know she's leaving again, and Ma laughs. But I tell you, I sit right in front of that suitcase for hours. Ma gets quite the kick out of this. I do this every time there is a suitcase. Call me crazy, I call me ready.

Well, the trip was an experience, I can assure you. I should tell you that when I am out in public, I have a different personality. I'm not sure why, but I become this coy, sweet, but snobby mutt. People seem to find this humorous, go figure. The good news for me about this trip was no kennel. First was the airplane. Oooeee, wouldn't want to do this too many times. I was in my little doggie bag and under the front seat where Ma was sitting. It was rather comfortable. Ma made sure that one of the windows faced her so I wouldn't get scared. My ride even had curtains! Costa Rica! What beautiful country! I can see why Ma loves it so.

So, Ma took me to this town called Santa Teresa, the roads to this town were awful, about three-hour drive from the ferry with bumps all the way, at night, in the rain. I have never been so glad to get somewhere. Thank the animal gods for air conditioning. When we arrived at this resort, there to greet us was a big baby dog that was very handsome. Ma says he was a golden lab. This lab took a liking to me and, although I was attracted to him, I couldn't let him know that and would turn my head every time he wanted to come near me. Can't let every Tom, Dick, and Rover think they can have me. Ma wasn't too pleased with my behavior, but she doesn't understand how dogs work. If you let them get too close, then you can't get rid of them. Right then was not a good time for me to have relationships. So, a girl does what she has to, doesn't she? But when he wasn't looking, I would watch him. He really was a cutie.

In front of our cottage, they had this get-up called a hammock. Well, was this cool or what? Ma would put me on this hammock and swing me over and over. This felt like I had gone to doggie heaven. See what I mean about having her wrapped around my little paw?

I saw these very weird things jumping around and I was so engrossed, never have I seen such a thing, hairy little beasts with feathers sticking out of their heads making the strangest noises, squawk, squawk squawk, going back and forth, back and forth on two very skinny feet that looked like forks. Ma informed me that these were chickens. Chickens, wow! Cute and goofy. Yet they sure got my attention. I spent hours watching those crazy kids. Got to really like them. I think of them a lot and miss them.

It was in Santa Teresa where I heard my first thunderstorm. Lordy, how do people survive these scary adventures? As soon as the thunder struck, I started shaking like a scaredy cat. Couldn't help it, freaked me out. Ma thinks this was touching. We had a moment of bonding, a woman and a dog, as she held me tight. This told me she had my back. I hate thunderstorms!

Had another adventure in Jaco, on the beach. I saw this enormous dog, I almost died. Right away, I began shaking and barking to let him know I was in control till Ma told me it wasn't a dog, but a horse! Wow, it was hard for me to wrap my head around that one. In a way, I was glad to hear it wasn't a dog cause then I wouldn't have to worry about him wanting to get too friendly with me, know what I mean?

So, here's a dorky thing to mention: Ma found these sun visors for dogs before we left Canada and thought they were sooo cute. Not only did she buy me a few, she started making them herself, so I had quite a collection of these things. Now to understand dogs, we don't like to wear anything, and most dogs find it very, very uncomfortable. I, on the other hand, kinda like it. What, with my colorful visors and my pink tongue sticking out a little, I knew I was adorable. The tongue sticking out is entertaining for humans for some reason. Dogs who are smart enough to do this get way more cookies than ones that don't. Having said this, I have to thank the animal gods she doesn't dress me up in dresses or stuff.

Anyways, people everywhere would laugh at me. Ma says it is laughter with love, not an insult, so I will believe her. From morning to night, all I heard was que linda, que linda, which means how beautiful! I had to work hard to not let that go to my head as Ma says I have quite an ego. One day a man said, "Que linda," and Ma said, "Who? Me or the dog?" He laughed, she laughed. Ma was once again tickled pink.

I notice it's the little things that makes Ma happy. She says she's always wanted to be a comedian but chose another path. She says she recalls exactly when she realized the power of humor. She was eight years old, in a courtroom testifying against her father for hurting her family. This she reminded me was a tough day in her life. She says her family, her mom, two sisters and others were all together in the courtroom and everyone looked so sad and on edge. Upon experiencing this, Ma started to tell jokes, although she couldn't remember any of them, except how everyone responded. Gone was the sadness, gone was the tension and the courtroom wasn't so scary, and she also liked the attention she got. So, she began to use humor as much as she could. She believes humor saved her life many times over.

I cry when I hear this, but Ma says do not do that cause she believes that everyone goes through tough circumstances in their life to learn powerful lessons, and we are given circumstances to help us to overcome obstacles related to our journey in life.

She calls these circumstances adversity. She says she played the victim for forty-one years and was thrilled when she learned she didn't have to be a victim anymore, that she could be a survivor, and she thought "Really." She believed, once a victim, always a victim! So, tears are not necessary for her. Gee, I love her when she talks like that.

She also tells kids when they come to her home that they have been given a gift being in a foster home. The looks she gets is funny. They certainly don't feel this is a gift. Then Ma tells them that's cause they are experiencing adversities at this very young age, and they feels like hardships, but they becomes strengths in their adult lives. She says other kids who haven't gone through adversity as youngsters will have a very hard time going through any adversity in adult life and it is to you, kids, that they will look to and ask you for advice. Kids love this. Don't get me wrong, there are a lot of kids who can handle adversity in adulthood. I am talking about the ones that have a hard time. Lots of kids don't need to be in foster homes to have that gift of surviving adversity. Too many factors to discuss.

Anyways, her foster kids laugh at her dorky jokes behind her back, but I know it's out of love for her, not insulting, cause she's so serious when she tries to be funny. By taking me to Costa Rica, she says I opened doors all over the place. She tells people that she didn't know you could have so much fun on a trip with a dog. Actually, she said mutt, but I let her know that I wasn't too thrilled with being labelled a mutt and she changed her word to honor my feelings. Nice eh? She also recognizes that labels really hurt people and that if we knew better, we would do better.

My ma loves to travel and has travelled a lot even by herself. She says sometimes it gets lonely, but she would rather have the travel experience than not. She always has a story about her trips. Two years ago, when she was in Hawaii, a cat befriended her. Apparently, this cat would sit outside her open patio door and sit and wait till he was verbally invited into her suite. She was so enamored with him, she spoiled him for days. He would travel through the tourist area for hours but always came to sleep at my ma's. She even has a photo of him. I asked her why she didn't bring him back to Canada.

"Are you kidding? This cat had it made in the shade on his journey." She wasn't foolish enough to believe she was the only one feeding him, and he seemed very happy in his travels, so why would she take him away from his paradise?

Ma says humans sometimes think rescuing is the right, spiritual thing to do, and their intentions are good intentions, but this is not always a good thing. Sometimes it can be a danger to the other party. She says, for example, interrupting a child's life journey. She says when you rescue a child from some silly thing, or big thing, he or she did, they never learn the real lesson they were meant to and the cost is always to the children, as their lessons are not gone, they pile up.

21

Did I mention Ma has a daughter named Winnie? Winnie is funny, she is Ethiopian. Huh? Ma says that means she is from Africa. Winnie came into our home when she was fifteen and fell in love with my ma. She could never say ma's name, Rennie, and would call her Rosie, and Ma thought this was the cutest thing.

Her name wasn't Winnie, either, when she came to live with us. Her name was Ewinniferig. When Ma heard that, she said, "No, your name is Winnie," and it stuck. Winnie loves it, so that's good. She really does look like a Winnie. So, one day Winnie asked my ma if she could call her mom. Ma was not comfortable with this and told her she would think about it. No one had ever asked her this and she says she always tells her new kids that she is "not" their mom, but a guide from this home to their next. As well, Ma didn't think she'd make a great mom. With too many triggers from the past, she didn't feel she had what it took to be a mom and didn't want to be a failure in Winnie's eyes. But, one day, in her meditation she understood that here was a girl with no mom who wanted one and wasn't that a gift God was giving her. And she could learn some lessons in this relationship that could be interesting. Look at the bright side, Ma thought, no diapers. Who could this possibly hurt?

So, she told Winnie yes. Winnie was elated and no more "Rosie." Although Ma missed that name, she admits she has a hard time to hear the word mom. She is smart enough to know this is a step on a path of her journey and knows that in time more will be revealed. Ma gets a big kick out of her. Especially when she teaches her Ukrainian. Winnie can hardly speak English, never mind Ukrainian, and Ma laughs and laughs. Winnie's coming into Ma's life also affected her whole family in many ways. Ma says it is interesting to experience different people's reactions to her and their relationship. The funniest thing is Winnie loves my ma's family and expresses it all the time. Now, Ma's family is quite dysfunctional, to say the least, and to hear someone say they love her family puts a smile on everyone's face. "Winnie," Ma said, "makes my day brighter, just by being in it." What a nice thing to say about someone.

Ma says Winnie should write a book; she has a story like Cinderella.

"Who is Cinderella?" I ask.

Ma said she would read me this story one day. "You know, Zoey, everyone has a story. The problem is as a society we don't take the time to listen."

Now Ma was taking me to meet Winnie. Even though Winnie was quite disappointed in Ma. Winnie believed Ma did not grieve enough for poor Hannah and promised my Ma that she will never love another dog. Till she met me, of course. Ma went to her apartment and had me in her sweater, hidden. Then she brought me out and put me in Winnie's hands and Winnie burst out crying. Wow. How crazy is that? She fell in love with me immediately.

Ma has a funny story to tell about Winnie. Winnie wanted to learn how to drive, so Ma decided to begin to teach her the basics. She took Winnie into her car and her first question to Winnie was "Winnie, point to the steering wheel," Winnie pointed to the gear shift. Ma said, "Winnie, get out of my f------g car." Ha ha ha. And Ma doesn't swear! I really like that story. Winnie gets very embarrassed when Ma tells the story, but you can see that she loves it. It took Winnie about twelve years to get her license, and Ma is very proud of her.

So, one year Ma took Winnie back to Ethiopia to see some of her relatives she hadn't seen in years. She says she will tell the story about Africa at another time but wanted to share one of her funniest stories now. Up and down the roads, or what they call roads, not paved, with mishmash huts all over the place, no signs on the huts, no numbers; it was ultra-confusing. And as she was being led to one hut for a visit and coffee, there was a hut with one cow inside. Ma was tickled pink. What cow in Canada gets their own home? She thought. She couldn't believe her eyes and took lots of pictures and, through the maze of huts, she kept seeing cows over the place. Apparently, they are important possessions to have, so they protect them from not being stolen. How cool is that?

Another time they were taking a walk down a road, and all of a sudden Ma heard wailing, loud and louder; it was coming from a white tent in the middle of the road. Winnie told her it was a mourning tent.

"A what?" I asked Ma.

"A mourning tent, when someone dies, they erect a large white tent in front of the dead person's house and folks come from all over, go into the tent and wail as much as they want, as long as it takes." Well, Ma not only loved it she says she put in her living will that she wants a mourning tent when she goes. As much as I don't like talk like that, I thought, this would suit my ma perfectly!

Baby Zoey

Jazzy

The pond

Promise

My favorite photo of Promise

Ms. Talula before first haircut

After Ms. Talula's first hair cut

Ms. T and Jag

Beautiful Costa Rica

Zoey and Baby Ms Talula

Ethiopian cow's home

Big Al my friend

My Ma with Zoey and Ms. Talula

Iguana on our patio Mexico

Ms Talula wins contest

Winnie Zoey and Ms Talula

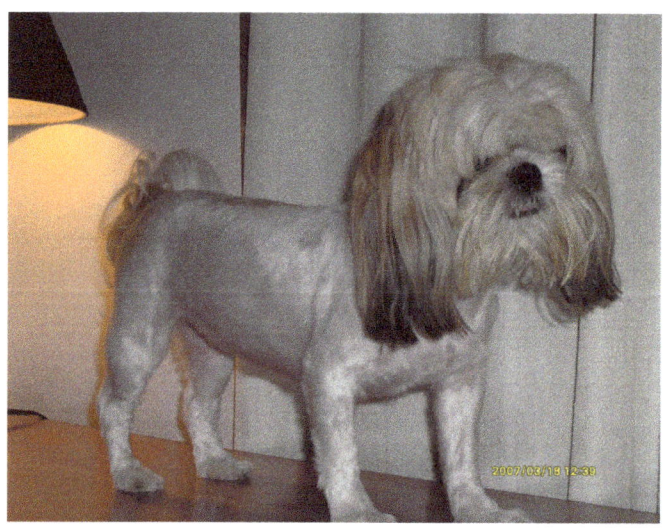

Costa Rican Lion cut

Mugs Malone

Hannah

22

Ma and I even got to go to Panama. O' boy, what a trip that was. There is a bridge called Sixaola Binational Bridge. It begins in a town called Sixaola in Costa Rica, and halfway over the bridge you are no longer in Costa Rica, you are now in a town called Guabito in Panama, the gateway to the Boca del Toro Islands. The road is an old elevated railroad grade. It is so old. Ma was so excited.

One little problem: people at customs wouldn't let me across cause my immigration papers were in my ma's room (yes, we dogs have our own papers), so they suggested Ma leave me on the sidewalk, tied to a pole, and go visit Panama without me. Ma was horrified at this suggestion, thank the animal gods, and refused to leave me. Then this nice lady came out, asked what the problem seemed to be and took us to see the big boss at customs and he took one look at me and said, "Que linda" … and allowed us into his country immediately with an escort! Pretty cool. I felt like royalty!

Ma took me to the Caribbean side of Costa Rica to a place called Puerto Viejo. I like that jungle feeling. She still hadn't found me a monkey; she had hoped she would see them here. We stayed at a place called Shawanda and it was beautiful. There wasn't even a TV and Ma was fine with that, surprise, surprise. Ma says she didn't realize she was addicted to TV till she came to Costa Rica and found out a lot of places don't have TV or have no cable, and two channels, only in Spanish, which my Ma doesn't understand well. Ha ha.

Anyways, this place had this wonderful porch and the sounds of the jungle surrounded us. They were majestic. I could hear the sounds of so many unknown animals it drove me a little crazy. I walked on that porch from one end to another, hour after hour, looking for these invisible noises. At night, there were these awful howls that really scared me. Ma would get all excited, "Zoey, those are the howler monkeys!" Yahoo, and off for a walk we would go at night, looking for what? Didn't see one howler monkey! Nor did we see any animals. I really felt bad for Ma cause she so wanted to see those animals. For the whole month we were there, we didn't see one monkey. Ma says it wasn't the time for us to see monkeys, says that she has faith in God's bigger picture and, even though she doesn't understand it, she accepts it and enjoys what is in front of her instead. She says she would be depressed, otherwise, about not seeing monkeys, and miss all the other gifts she as receiving. Sometimes she says this is hard to do but continues to work at it cause it makes her life easier and happier. She says life happens to all of us, and how we react to what life has to offer is the key. I like that concept. "Where can we get more keys? I will keep watching for this key and let you know."

I was really mad at my ma one day at this nice place in Jaco. Ma was at the swimming pool when she heard a splash, and low and behold a small iguana had fallen from a tree into the pool. I had never seen an iguana and was sorry to have missed it cause Ma had me chained to our porch out of the pools view, till I remembered what Ma had said about the monkeys: if I was meant to see them, I would. Then I got over myself! So, Ma got one of the groundskeepers to fish him out of the pool. Ma did get photos of this, and I'm happy the iguana was OK and got to live another day.

I got sick in a town called Puntarenas. I had an ear infection and Ma had to find an animal doc to look at it. She had this nice taxi driver who knew such a doc and took us right to him. Ma's fear was that Costa Ricans think that dogs are like cows, and they cannot understand the crazy relationships North Americans have with their dogs. They would never dream of letting them sleep on their bed … yikes. This is information I could have lived without. When we got to the animal doc's office it was in what we Canadian's would call a garage, he put me on this table and verified I indeed had an ear infection. He then proceeded to give me a needle right between my back legs. O' my loving animal gods, what the heck does that place have to do with my ear? Even Ma looked worried. He then gave me another shot, some ointment and some pills. Again, with the pills! Ma says what really surprised her was the cost compared to Canada. In Costa Rica the cost was a fraction of what Ma would have paid in Canada. "O, goodie, I'm thinkin, another silver lining in a time of pain". And yes I am being facetious! "Impressive word, eh?"

The first time Ma gave me the pill, I threw right up in a nice restaurant, not an ideal place to throw up. Ma cleaned me up and the floor as good as she could and rushed me out of that restaurant, never to return. She was so embarrassed.

She threw out the pills, realizing they were way too strong for me and used the ointment, thank the animal gods. Good news was it worked. Ma's pretty smart. I'm really happy to say, that was the only time I got sick in Costa Rica.

23

"A month later, home we went. O'boy, it felt good to be home. I forgot how nice home is. As a dog I was surprised I could feel these emotions. And I was sure happy to see Promise and Jazzie again. My tail was waggin, Jazzie's tail was wagging and even Promise had a wag in his tail! I understand now when Ma says that travelling can be hard work, yikes.

Most unfortunate was going back to dog food. I am so envious of people who have the variety of food to choose from compared to us dogs and cats. People, please listen to me: I believe as long as you give us a balanced diet, we could eat your food. So please, people, do some soul-searching and homework about what we can and cannot eat. There are a lot healthier options than boring dog food. Take it from me, we would thank the animal gods from here to eternity.

Actually, a few months back, there was a recall on a list of dog and cat food and, apparently, the world had never seen anything like this, and people began to look into their hearts and ask themselves, "What the heck are we feeding Fido?" This is a very good question to ask yourself about someone you claim to love. She says it's a wonderful opportunity God gives us when something like that recall happens. I can assure you that there were many happy barks and meows going on all over the world that month. I do notice that Ma is feeding Jazzie and me a lot tastier treats since then. All one can do is pray.

I am so sad to say Jazzie was not feeling well. An earache, again. Ma took him to the animal doctor and found out he has brain cancer. O' my lord. Ma was in shock. She and the doc talked about surgery for him, and the doc said it was really was not a possibility considering where the cancer is located. His chances of survival were not good; they wouldn't even attempt it. Ma brought Jazzy home and we loved him up. The energy in our home once again changed. There was this sadness all about us. Ma now had a decision to make.

Unknown to us, Ma had been planning to go to Costa Rica for three months. She had everything arranged and even had a worker set up to move into our home. So, changing the schedule would be mega hard. And she did not want to leave Jazzie with strangers. Especially being sick. She knew she needed to let him go. She says the day she took him to the animal doctor to say good-bye, it was the first time Jazzie did not howl in the car. Which shocked my Ma. This told her Jazzie knew where she was going, and it broke Ma's heart. It still amazes her how smart dogs really are. She held him in her arms as he went to his demise and o' boy the tears. She tried to tell us what happened, but we wanted to know where he was and why wasn't he home, and mad at Ma for leaving him somewhere. All we knew was this empty feeling energy in the home without Jazzie which was felt by all the kids and me and Promise. It was amazing. I am so happy that I got to spend all that time with Jazzie. I will miss him terribly. Ma says that's what happens when a new kid arrives or leaves. The energy constantly changes. Sometimes good, sometimes not so much. I am going to have to pay attention to this energy thing.

She also said there is a silver lining in all sadness.

"Really, Ma?"

Ma said, "Remember Jazzie's love for Hannah? O' yeah. Well, guess who Jazzie is meeting at the Pearly Gates right now as we speak? That's right. Hannah."

O' my lord, that is a silver lining. My sadness is almost gone. I have tears of joy. Ma really believes in the journey of passing on to the hereafter, all your past pets are there to greet you as well as past friends and relatives. The ones you like, of course.

24

About a month before we left, I was busy in our courtyard garden doing garden things when, out of the blue, a voice spoke to me! No, I was not on drugs, high or drunk. But for those who have heard that voice, you know it is heaven sent. It was deep and loving, and His message was short, he said, "Write your book through Zoey's eyes." Well, I looked around and thought, Oh my God. What happened? I have often asked God, speak to me, God, I need your advice, God, now would be good, God. His advice never came in sound, if that makes sense? When you do "hear" something from the God, it simply takes your breath away. To be honest, I have tried and tried to explain the glory of this and cannot state this anymore eloquently than this.

I wasn't thinking about books at the time, although I have tried to write my memoir lots of times. The problem was I could not put the Rennie Essence into writing. I talk with my hands; it's the Ukrainian in me, and I make funny faces when I tell a story. That just didn't translate on my computer, making it all sound so boring, so I gave up, years ago.

When I heard His voice, I couldn't help but think that gods do pay attention to our wishes. I once again went into a delayed reaction. I was so blown away with the humbleness of this moment, I had to sit with it a while.

It's like if a million dollars falls into your lap, right out of the blue. You know something magical just happened, yet you cannot believe that you are the recipient of such a gift. I didn't tell anyone for a long time about this divine gift. I did go on the computer a few days later and began to type and, wouldn't you know it, the flow was there, all because I could speak through a dog! I found that both our essences showed up! I kept writing and writing. How exciting. Big, big daily gratitude to God!

# # #

Ma bought a laptop to take to Costa Rica and her fantasy was to write a book about me in the jungle amongst the monkeys. Now she told us about her next adventure and, yes, she was taking me! Yahoo. I saw she had dragged out my luggage and right away I knew I was going. Boy, was I excited; she took that bag out a month before we left and every day I'd think, when the heck are we going? Well, the day finally came and off we went.

This time in the airports in Vancouver and in Houston, Ma did not close the top on my luggage, and I got to lie right on top of it, watching all the people. It was so, so cool, I can tell you. People were laughing and laughing at me. Ma says cause I was so well behaved, didn't jump out once, and Ma says I looked like the star that I sometimes think I am. Hmm.

Many people came over and commented to Ma about my behavior and Ma was really proud of me. She says she wants to decorate my luggage and call it "Pimp My Ride" … I do not like the sounds of that. I told you she was weird. Not once did security come and tell her to close the bag and that made me very happy, never mind my ma, cause when we took the ferry from the Island to Vancouver, Ma had to close my bag and even my windows and, let me tell you, she had never done that before. I was sooo scared that I peed in my bed, I'm embarrassed to say. Ma, being the compassionate person she is, took care of that and hugged me even more, taking away my shame. Ma says it's cause dogs on ferries have to go into this little cold room by all the cars and Ma doesn't like that room, so that's why she sneaks me into people population. I think that is a stupid rule. Who are we hurting when we are zipped up in a bag? Anyways, I don't want to go through that again, golly, the fear.

One of the results of being spoiled in the airports was this: when we got to Costa Rica, I kinda got lazy and didn't want to walk. I liked being driven or carried; it suits me! Ma gets pretty aggravated with me, especially when we are in the middle of the street. I tell you I am a very stubborn doggie when I want to be and pretty strong if I do say so myself. Ma is amazed at my stubbornness. Once again, I got the "look." Ma says she gets so angry when I do this, yet at the same time, happy that I haven't got us both killed! I will work on this.

Anyways, it was nice to be back in Costa Rica. We travelled around to a few resorts and guess what I saw? Monkeys. And lots of them. Wow, these kids were hilarious. They travelled in troupes and seemed not to have any fear of me. They even came onto our patio, with me there, and could not have cared less. I was absolutely amazed, thought my eyes were gonna pop out of my head, but I didn't chase them or anything cause I was so enamored with them. They love bananas and the resort always fed them. As Ma was feeding a bunch, they began to get very aggressive, and Ma was really surprised. She watched them snarl as they grabbed pieces of the banana before she could break them off. One lady from Europe gave my Ma a talking to, she said it was not nice to feed the monkeys and that Ma was killing them. Ma immediately stopped and spent the evening feeling very ashamed.

She could not understand why bananas were not a good thing for monkeys as it was a fruit. Aren't fruits natural? So, the next day she went to the local vets and asked the animal doc why it was bad. Well, the doc had a lot to say, the most important being that bananas are sprayed with some kind of disinfectant or insecticide, whatever that means, doesn't sound so appealing, before it reaches humans, and this insecticide can kill the monkeys. They can even catch diseases from a human's hand. Wow.

Also, when you feed them, sometimes they get aggressive towards humans and other animals. Never mind interfering with their natural habitat, yada yada … I can tell you, Ma will never feed another monkey, but oh, how hard it is when you see those adorable little furry gifts … _ like the ants and chickens, I could watch these kids for hours too. Now I understand my ma's love for them.

In Dominical, there was this beautiful resort with casitas surrounded by jungle. the casita patios were wrapped in white gauze; this was Ma's idea of camping, but it was short lived. The resort had a rule: no dogs allowed. Can you believe that?

Well, did I mention Ma does not take no very lightly? Kind of like me. So, she asked to speak to the boss and convinced him that I, Zoey, would behave myself. And that I had character references. A dog with character references? Anyways, the boss looked at me, and I knew he was thinking, "Que linda." Then he agreed and stated that if he got even one complaint, we were out ... whoohoo! No complaints, I can assure you!

One evening I was lying on our patio while Ma was watching TV, and this huge thing walked by. I ran to Ma and she saw my eyes and came running. We had this silent communication between us that is very cool.

Smart, aren't I? Anyways, this animal was huge; it had this long thick snout and furry tail, and Ma found out it was a baby ant eater. "Baby, my ass, oops, sorry." I would have been scared to see the parents. Anyways, Ma was sooo excited to see this animal, as she never had seen one before, she grabbed her camera. Her hands were so shaky, she couldn't get the shot, which is really sad cause this ant eater was walking really, really slow. Ma says he was even slower than Auntie Patti. Ha ha. Ma says she has to learn patience, a downfall in her learning. Every day after, she looked for these exotic animals and didn't see another, so simply enjoyed the pleasure of seeing anything at all.

*Next stop was this hotel in Manuel Antonio again. O' lord, this place was the worst and, apparently, quite expensive, although I don't know why. We were on the second floor with lots of windows, looking into the jungle, but the windows didn't open. All we had was an air conditioner, and the humidity was a killer. Not only that, every time I had to go to the bathroom, we had to go down all these steps an*d

I couldn't go on any grass cause there wasn't any! As well, it was the rainy season and all there was, was mud … yikes. I do not like mud, I can assure you.

So, Ma had to take me to the street which was half a block from our room, and did I mention that the sidewalks are really, really tiny, so you have to be very, very careful not to get hit by a car?

My thought was, who the heck can pee under these conditions? I refused to go, I mean, really. The next day I was as sick as a dog, excuse the pun. Ma knew she had to do something and cause it was Christmas season, the hotel people would not give her any money back. That one day cost my ma over $900. Wow, even to a dog that sounds like a lot, but Ma loves me. She will tell you it was all worth it. Aww, Ma!

25

Ma called this apartment she had reserved for the next stop in our stay and she told them our sad story, and they offered us our apartment early without charge. Ma said, "See, life always balances out, so never worry too much, not worth it." Now we are at the apartment and guess what? They have two dogs, very big and mean dogs. One is a German Shepherd that is six years old and his name is Oso, which means bear in Spanish, and the other dog is a Siberian Husky, who is one year old and his name is Rocky. Rocky had the bluest eyes and they were not kind eyes, they were intense and piercing. I was so wary of him for some reason. He really scared me and anyways, who has a Husky in tropical weather? Felt sorry for this mutt, and the heat he must have felt. They were called guard dogs. Now, this did not make me feel too secure. Why would we need guard dogs? After a few days or should I say nights, I understood why: amongst the fireworks were gun shots. Yikes! Ma says there are a lot of robberies of foreigners' properties and the security people have to sometimes shoot to scare these robbers away, "Good going, Ma, nice place to take me."

And these dogs…o' animal gods, am I ever going to like dogs? Please help me to not be such a snob, animal gods, and maybe I can have friends like my ma. But not with these ones. The worst one is Rocky and, thank the animal gods, he knows I don't like him and stays away from me. Ma laughs. She says he is scared of little ol' me. Now the other one, Oso the bear, is not sooo bad; he certainly isn't scared of me and has taken a shine to my ma. He goes right past me to her; he doesn't care if I bark at him or nothing. It's actually a little intimidating. Oso goes over to my ma, gives her a big kiss on her face and literally falls down beside the bed and goes to sleep. The nerve. I see the chuckles in my ma's eyes, and believe me when I say, I am not chuckling. She really has to stop giving them cookies.

Did I mention that in our backyard there were a lot of monkeys to be seen? They fly from tree to tree and Ma watched them for hours. Squirrel monkeys, capuchin monkeys, even howler monkeys and was she excited. Being on the ground, I couldn't see them, so the pleasure is all my ma's. To give her credit, she would put me on the top of the stairwell, and I thought I saw some, but my concentration is a dog's, not a human's. Couldn't follow them so fast.

After a month, Ma was getting way bored. Did I mention she likes to be on the move? Likes new vistas, new people, new experiences. She says it's cause when she was little, she moved around a lot, when she was in those places called foster homes. One year she went to seven different schools. "Wow," she said. Moving is gratifying and easy for her and doesn't bother her, although she says as she is getting older, moving is taking a bigger toll on her (whatever that means). She says it's harder to find the energy to make new close friends and

*that although she does have some key friends in many places,
she says there is no friend like an old friend. Huh.*

It's all good cause she's got me.

*After a month or so, yup, she got bored. So, she decided
to quit smoking. Now to know my Ma, this wasn't something
I wanted to hear. From what I know, and have heard from
Jazzie and Promise, is that this road is a dangerous one for
anyone standing in her way. She has tried many, many times
and failed. She went to a doctor and got some pills that helped
her quit. Thank the gods.*

*A couple of weeks in, she took me to the animal doc she
liked cause she spoke English and was pretty and kind. Twice
before, she had this doc give me a bath and groom me and
the doc did a really nice job. This time, Ma wanted me to
have a hair trim. Trim being the magic word. If you look at
the front cover, that is what I looked like going in. What Ma
said to this vet was to give Zoey a little pocito haircut. Even
showed her how little she wanted it trimmed. Somewhere, in
this conversation, interpretation of the word "pocito" got lost
in translation, big time! This, she reminds me, is why, if you
want to live in another country that speaks Spanish, learn
Spanish! When Ma came to pick me up, she was horrified at
what they had done to me! Even the doc must have felt bad
cause she wouldn't come out. I got what they call the lion
cut. Sounds nice, I promise you it was not. Ma said saying it
was a lion cut is an insult to lions everywhere. Just my face
had hair, the rest of my body was entirely shaved. Personally,
I felt pretty good, ravishing as a matter of fact. I couldn't
understand the shock in Ma's eyes cause I couldn't see behind
me, thank the animal gods. When we got home, she began to
walk in circles crying, "Why Zoey, God, why?" Something*

in that mournful lament puzzled me. I'm thinkin Ma has seriously lost her mind and maybe she should light up a smoke to relax. Just sayin!.

She says she eventually came to the conclusion that her God was testing her, and now was the time to find her humor. Remembering what she learned in AA, "what's not in your control, let go." So she tried to let go of this shock.

I was fine with my haircut. If she needed humor, well, knock yourself out ma"

Poor Zoey, I tried really hard to not show her how embarrassed I was to be walking around with this goofy goofy lookin mutt. It wasn't her fault. And she actually looked kind of pleased with herself. The fool!

The next week, we went to the front to check out the sunset and accidentally didn't close the gate fast enough. Out flew Oso and Rocky. Now the drama began. Our street was filled with dogs of all sizes, not on leashes, and resting and enjoying their neighborhood when these two animals rushed to the closest ones to them and began eating them! God's truth. Ma began to panic, dogs were screaming, my Ma was screaming, the two mutts would not listen to her as they were enjoying dinner! It was mayhem. Finally, a man next door came out and started throwing bricks at them, Ma was again horrified, crying and yelling, "Don't kill them, stop them, but don't kill them." The man clearly wanted them dead. Ma was truly beside herself; the scene was awful, and she could hear the cries of the little dogs being eaten. Thank God I stayed behind in our yard and, boy, was I scared. After about five harrowing minutes, the owner of Oso and Rocky came out and got them back inside the yard. Ma was so upset and angry — why didn't this man come out when he first heard the commotion? "No habla ingles."

And Ma didn't smoke. Again, she knew she was being tested by God and again was very proud of herself. Our travels were winding down. We were becoming tired.

26

Soon it was time to go home again. Ma was in a very good space. She knew she would not be moving to Costa Rica and was excited to come home and move on with her life. Three months away made her grateful to have a home to go to. She realized in these three months that moving to Costa Rica was a fantasy, not a reality. Here is her example: Remember she bought a laptop computer and was going to start my book? And she was so excited? Ma says she and I were going to live in the jungle, she, to write my book and me, play with monkeys. Then, the first day she was there one of the workers in the resort told her that she had better hide her laptop in the daytime as it would surely be stolen, otherwise. Ma was so very disappointed. She had to write at night indoors as there are too many mosquitos at night. It took away her enthusiasm to write this book. Now, I'm depressed.

Another example: she was looking for a small resort to buy. This would be her bread and butter while living there. I was quite sad to hear this, and she asked me why, and I told her that she deserved far more than bread and butter. She laughed and laughed.

Apparently, when the wife heard that she was looking for property, hers became available. The owner was a Costa Rican guy who couldn't control his dogs. His wife was very feisty gal from Italy. She was the deal maker. So, she gave Ma a price and it was in her ballpark, so she got really excited. There were like three suites in the back and her own personal apartment in the front with a very bid yard, where Ma thought she could have two casitas built as well as a swimming pool. Perfect. We could watch monkeys all day long, forever! She was smart enough to talk with a Costa Rican engineer from her AA group in Manuel Antonio who came to check out the place. He didn't even go into the house and told her "no." What the heck. Here's the reality: there is a Costa Rican law that you cannot build anything that has water near it, and at the end of the big yard was a water stream. So, no pool, no casitas. Ma was so disappointed. She talked to the lady and the lady said, "No problem, we fix." Ma says when someone tells you that, run!

If she knew Spanish, it would have helped a lot but, as well, in the three months we were there, she was always treated as a tourist and felt constantly on guard fearing being robbed or hurt. This was not Ma's idea of retirement! Ma had been coming here for years and noticed that, in the beginning, there were concrete fences around properties with broken glass, to protect the property from robbers. Now, years later, it is so bad that a lot of homes now have 24-hour guards. This is so unsettling for Ma. She says being a single, white female doesn't help. So, back home, it was

27

When we arrived home, Ma decided she was going to get a new puppy. Good thing I didn't hear that, I would not have been thrilled. Ever since she saw the movie, **As Good as It Gets**, she fell in love with the puppy they had on the show. She didn't even know what kind of breed it was, but as luck would have it, while we were in Costa Rica, she met a woman who had the same kind of dog, and it was called a Brussels Griffon.

So, the story goes, these dogs come from Belgium and were the first dogs to be bred for human companionship. Ooh. Not only that, they were considered "monkey" dogs. For goodness sake, I am stuck with monkeys for the rest of my life. Can't get away from them. Not only that, when she got on the internet, she learned that these dogs are very hard to get, but no, not for Ma. There was one female available right here in BC, up in the north. Of course, Ma bought her, and this little Brusslels Griffon was shipped and flown to Victoria. I have to be honest here: I hated her. I tried and tried, and I was so angry at Ma that I avoided her for two months. No kisses, no smiles, no happy tails. Ma has a picture of us; she says one picture speaks a thousand words on how I felt. See *for yourself. I know, I'm a little stubborn. But darn, this pup was not only goofy but wouldn't stay away from my ma. Ma agreed, she was definitely the oddest looking dog she had ever gotten,* but the pup had such personality. Huh?

Did I mention there was the vet's yearly contest. Cats and dogs, kittens and puppies, and who do you think came in second prize for puppy? That's right, Ms. Talula with a dandelion in her mouth, Ma caught this kodak moment in the courtyard. Apparently, she's not too smart in the nutrition area!

Ma says she went outside her comfort zone to get this breed cause usually she likes fluffy dogs and this one was far from fluffy. Ma named her Ms. Talula. What kind of dumbass name is that? She named her after an actress in the '40s named Talula Bankhead. Yeah, the '40s. That's where she belonged as far as I was concerned.

For some reason she got tons of attention. Ma was laughing every day, which made me even angrier. She tried to explain to me that I was her Zen dog and Ms. Talula was her humor dog. And she loved us both, and was so sad to see me go through my depression that she even went to the animal doc to ask if she should give Ms. Talula away, she was worried I would begin to get sick, I was so unhappy. The animal doc told her "no way," that having Ms. Talula was good for me cause obviously I was having "attachment disorder." Huh! When I heard Ma tell me that, I began to get over myself and slowly bonded with this goofy-looking monkey dog. I was very touched that Ma had even considering giving Ms. Talula away for me. So, Ma started to teach me about boundaries. Believe me, I had a lot. I knew this would be a slow process, and Ma says that was fine as long as I was moving forward.

Even when we went to the beach, if someone knew Ms. Talula's breed they would say, "Oh, is that a Brussels Griffon?" and Ma would be all delighted, and if they didn't know her breed, they would say, "Oh, rescue." Ha ha. This dog was so bad, Ma had to take her to two schools, kindergarten and grade one and two. Ha ha, I thought, I didn't have to go to school. I was feeling a little superior right there, but then Ms. Talula could do all these tricks that were really impressive, and Ma was tickled pink. Once again, I felt left out.

When Ms. Talula was bad, Ma called her Ms. Mugly. Now that's a name that should have stuck… OK, I'm sorry, I can still get a touch jealous at times. I am, after all, a dog without tools like you humans. Now, this mutt had all these challenges, towel challenged, comb challenged, paper challenged, children challenged, backpack challenged, hat challenged, geez, this mutt was plain "challenged."

And to all you motorcycle drivers out there, be on the look-out for this mutt. As soon as she sees a bike, she barks out of nowhere real loud and scares the bejesus out of them. Ma's worried she is going to cause one of these bikers to have an accident.

And still my ma is humored by Ms. Talula and her peculiarities. When Ms. Talula gets spooked, her whole face goes nuts. Her eyes look like devil eyes, and her growl could scare a German Shepherd. Ma thought this was so funny, she had her videotaped and put on You Tube! Now, I am telling you, she has never put me on YouTube. I don't know how I am going to lighten up here, but I have to try.

One day, one of Ma's boys came up to her, after living with her for three months and asked her, "What is that white dog's name?"

Ma said, "You have lived here for three months and still you do not know her name?"

The boy replied, "For three months, all I ever hear around here is Ms. Talula, Ms. Talula." Ha ha.

'See, am I lyin? now you know why I am so put off.'

We almost lost Ms. Talula when she was, like, five months old. Ma had us in the car, me on the passenger seat and Ms. Talula in her lap, she pulled into a mini mart and Ms. Talula climbed up and jumped out the window. It played out in slow motion. When Ms. Talula landed on the concrete parking lot, she shook her silly self off, looked around, and must have thought, woohoo, look at this playground, as it was a large parking lot, and began to run right toward a main road. Ma started screaming, another lady near the store was screaming, and Ms. Talula ran on.

"Guess she didn't learn too much in school, eh?" At the very last moment, inches before Ms. Talula reached the busy road, for some reason Ma yelled out, "Cookies!" and this nutty monkey dog stopped on a dime, turned around and ran towards Ma … Ma was so angry with her and could not show it, and had to give her a cookie. Even I was shaken up with all this drama. And now she laughs!

One day Ma took both of us to the beach, which we loved. Right on the Pacific Ocean. You could run free and we loved that. On this day there was this grey, grey fog that was incredible; you could not see where the sky ended, and the ocean started. Both Ms. Talula and I ran into this fog with Ma coming behind us, when out of the fog, like a very scary movie, came two pit bulls right towards us! That's right, folks, pit bulls! Now, lord knows there is a lot of debate about these dogs, are they dangerous or are they trained badly? Ma says there are so many stories out there about the locking jaws of a pit bull. Once they get a bite, there is no letting go. The other matter about the pit bull is you cannot trust them. So, many people say, "Oh, he has never bitten a soul, loves people and other animals, plays with my grandchildren."

Guess what? Judge Judy gets letters all the time from folks who have been terrorized, their grandchildren losing eyes, faces scarred for life or worse cause of the nice pit bull that is "wonderful" with children. So, Ma's opinion is if you cannot trust a dog, it needs to go, period! She says it is a pit bulls' nature to attack. You can have one for five years and one day the granddaughter pulls his tail, he's in a bad mood and "attack." Life changing! Is that scary enough to "not" get a pit bull? There are so very many breeds to choose from.

So, back to this story, out of the fog comes these two pit bulls running towards me and Ms. Talula, straight on. One is brown and one is white with a caged muzzle on, meaning she can't bite anyone. Well there's a red ole flag. Well, you would think that the muzzle is a very good thing, can't hurt anyone, can he? Ma rushed to Ms. Talula who still a puppy and knows no boundaries involving other dogs, loves them all and grabbed him up. But no, forget Ms. Talula, the white one with the caged muzzle came right for me! He jumped on me and in seconds was burying my head in the sand. Ma was horrified, ran up to this dog screaming at the owner to get this dog off me. The owner was a young girl approximately twenty years old. She jumped on this white pit bull and got him off me, then she began to hit this pit bull over and over while she dragged him back to her car. Ma's heart was torn. She was so happy that I seemed OK, but so sad to see this pit bull getting beaten up. Ma says she almost had a heart *attack. She could not catch her breath and had to sit down and slowly breathe. The funny part was, I was fine, didn't shake, didn't cry, no PTSD. I'm still not sure why I wasn't upset with this. Absolutely out of character for me. Ma says it was like a movie, a very quick movie, but a movie anyways. Stay away from pit bulls with muzzles on, folks.*

28

Ma suddenly began buying new everything. She says since she was not moving to another country, she needed some change. I hear folks say that she was going through "the change." Huh? She really went all out. Got a new bed, new renovations on the house, new floors, skylights, a real spending spree. She looked like she was enjoying it. And she started smoking again.

"No comment from the dog's house."

Then she decided to get a new car. Her old car was not old, only thirty-five clicks and looked like new. She traded it in for a sporty two-door coupe called the Infinity, even had tinted windows. Ma loved starting it up and the sound of the engine, said it purred. What did she get? A "cat car." She got such a kick every time she started it up.

It wasn't long before she realized the mistake she made. To begin, she had to get all new tires for snow, now that costs a lot, then realized two doors was a pain (you know where) every time she took us dogs or the kids out. And last but not least, those tinted windows, she could hardly see out of them. Ha ha. She thought she would feel like a cool ca. See, there's the cat thing!

Her eyes are getting tired and forget driving at night. Ha ha. So, one day soon after that, she traded the Infinity for another; this time a Jag.

Well now, this was a nice car, even I liked it. Ma says she had always wanted one and she enjoyed the ownership of it for over a year. She says she realized it was an expensive car to own and her ego no longer needed that kind of attention and there was a downside to owning one, people charged you more for stuff when they saw your Jag and repairs were outrageous.

So, gone was the Jag; she traded it in for a nice reliable brand-new Mazda six with four doors, no tinted windows and a really good warranty on it.

29

OMG (yes, Ma is teaching me computer speak), what a year this has been for us. Life has turned 360 degrees and it ain't over yet. Time has flown by. "O'no ma says, time doesn't move, time stands still, we humans move through time". *O'boy here we go.*

Ma said, "In life and the workplace, there is always a hierarchy."

Yes, I had to ask, "What is a hierarchy?"

"A system of grades of authority ranked one above another!"

Huh?

Ma says, for example, in a restaurant, the owner is the top of the hierarchy and the floor cleaner is probably the lowest in this hierarchy. Or it could be the waitress or the dishwasher. The point being there is always someone beneath the owner's status. "Are you with me here, Zoey?"

"Yes ma'am, I hear you." In fostering, Ma views the hierarchy as follows: The top is always the government in charge, then administrators, office managers, social workers, and then at the bottom is the foster parent. Now, here is the scary part for the foster parent: If anything goes

wrong, as it often does, the last one on the totem pole usually pays the price and that person is the foster parent.

"What, Ma, is a totem pole? Dare I ask?"

"A totem pole is a post with carved and painted symbols or figures." *"Of course it is.*

One of my biggest worries as a foster parent is being sued. They say you are not a real foster parent until you have allegations against you. When allegations happen, you are called into the office and questioned by a social worker about the allegation. If it is a small thing, it just gets written up in your file. If it is bigger, then your home could be closed and worse. Here is one of my examples.

A social worker called me on the phone to say we needed a meeting immediately as one of my kids told her I was selling drugs to other kids in my home. What? A meeting was held at my home with the kid, the social worker, my resource worker, a mental health worker, and the process went like this.

Johnie (not real name), how do you know Rennie sells drugs to the kids in her home? Asked his social worker. I waited with bated breath. Johney said, "Rennie gave Ron (not real name) money for his clothing allowance. As she does every month for every kid. Johnie claims that Ron did not buy clothes, he bought drugs instead, so Rennie bought him drugs." "Really!"

The social worker said to Johnie, "Oh, Johney, you are having a bad day, aren't you?" You think Johnie is having a bad day? Hello!

"Not one of these workers apologized to me. They just moved on, never mind that I had lost a week's sleep with worrying and anxiety!" That is one allegation.

The second situation is too funny to not include here. There was a girl we will call Sandy. She was only with me a few weeks, and I could tell she didn't bond with us, which was fine as I have an open- door policy that if you don't like me or this home, just let me know and we can move you elsewhere. No problem. I guess Sandy didn't get this memo. One day her social worker called to say she received an allegation from Sandy. Oh lord, I thought, now what. Sandy told her social worker that I walk around the house in my bra and panties all the time. This just got me laughing so hard. Here's the reason:

As an incest survivor, one of my hang-ups is body image. Most of my life I have tried to hide my body with baggy clothes. Which bugs me these days. I had such a nice body and never knew it. Anyways, I even had trouble viewing myself in the mirror.

As a teenager, I banned the bra! Yes, those were the hippy days. And what fun! We had the best music ever! One of my biggest regrets is not going to see Elvis Presley! Sob, sob. Not wearing a bra was not a big deal to me as I was considered small and I wore baggy clothes that didn't show anything. Ha ha. Now having said this, I have never walked around my home in my underwear! When the social worker asked me about this allegation, I simply told her honestly that I had not worn a bra since I was sixteen. End of allegation, and Sandy got her wish and was moved to another foster home.

Here's a funny story about my body shame. When I was married for about six years, I was in the shower when I noticed a tick on my breast. You bet I yelled like crazy and my hubby came running into the shower room to see

what was wrong. I told him, "Look I have a tick, get it off."
He just stood there looking. I said, "What are you doing?"
He said, "It's been years and I have never seen you naked
in the daylight." … ha ha.

30

After allegations is the dreaded lawsuit. To be hit by one of these is life changing. And not in a good way.

In the area of fostering and dealing with the government as your boss, if you are sued, it quickly becomes a very lonely and confusing time. For the first time in my life, I was being sued! This chapter is strictly sharing my opinion and experience about this lawsuit. By no means am I looking for retaliation or revenge. I just want to share my story, which I believe needs to be shared for there are many stories like mine that never comes out because governments get to hide behind confidentiality clauses, which force us to say nothing.

There are facts here I will not be sharing as I do not want to make this about any individual involved with this lawsuit. This isn't about them. This is my story, it's about me. For all foster parents who have experienced being sued as a foster parent, this chapter is for you.

The one positive here was I belonged to the Foster Parent Association and they were a great resource considering there was now no one at my office I could talk to. I also was granted a lawyer, no expense to me, which

I know is a huge expense. It at least was one thing that I didn't have to worry about. Foster parents, if you do not belong to Foster Parents Association, do it now!

And may I take this opportunity to acknowledge this lawyer and thank him for his amazing commitment to me and my wellbeing. I could call him at any time, and he was there for me. He became invaluable to me throughout the long, long process. You know who you are. From my heart, I can never thank you enough.

This new claim involved one of my kids and the incident didn't even happen in my home. Now, I cannot divulge a lot as there are so many confidentiality rules here that I respect.

This lawsuit hurt my soul. I am a foster parent. I have homed over 250 teens. I love them. Once the lawsuit is filed, you are immediately a pariah. Before Zoey could ask, I said, "A pariah is a social outcast." I was now alone. I could not speak to my resource worker, or any worker through the office I had a contract with. I was ostracized from all of them. *"What does ostracize mean, Ma?"*

"Ostracized means 'exclude from society'." The suddenness with which this happens takes your breath away. Suddenly, there was a new normal in my life and it was absolutely frightening.

My home was not closed to fostering; I still had three other teens to tend to. The lawsuit was not something I could share with them. I needed to be my old, normal self when they were around as that was important to me. Kids never need to deal with adult issues. Anxiety began to set in. I attended more AA meetings around this time as I knew that was where the love and trust was and knew I would need serious support. Big gratitude for these angels.

A year in, I began throwing up; the stress was obvious. Even the house had strange energy in those days. To add to this dysfunctional home, I had some tough kids to deal with. Life was certainly taking a toll on me. What I was experiencing and didn't know at the time was burnout. Every foster parent knows what this term means. I was burning out.

31

Through all the stress Ma had, I became nicer to Ms. Talula, so she wouldn't have an added stress over our relationship as well. I know Ma was very grateful for this. Ma probably doesn't even notice, but I do pay attention to Ms. Talula's holistic wellbeing. I know Ms. Talula was grateful, as she'd began sniffing my bottom over and over in gratitude, for God's sakes.

There came a day in early spring she got a phone call from a social worker about some criticism over handling a situation with a kid. Usually she handles criticism as a learning curve. No learning curve attitude here! She felt she was being bullied by this worker and something changed for her in that moment.

She says this worker's comments were the straw that broke the camel's back. "What the heck does that mean?" Trust me when I say we do not have any camels in my house! I didn't ask, thinkin now didn't seem like a good time. Looked like she had enough to think about. I'm thinkin she has lost her ever-lovin mind is what I am thinkin.

So, Ma put on her thinking cap again. I still haven't found that cap! She decided she would sell our beautiful home *and take Ms. Talula and me to Mexico for a year! Thank you, animal God's. See, now she even has me thankin the God's. She says she feels this is a great opportunity and to take advantage of it.*

A year! Yahoo! Then she would come back, buy a smaller home and foster two kids after the lawsuit was over. Fostering four kids at a time would be no more. Getting too old, she says. She said even professors and highly educated people had what they call sabbaticals, and she was gonna have one, even though she is not a teacher. I notice her humour is coming back already. How exciting this has become. The tides feel like they are changing.

32

Ma listed her house, and the next week she and her friend Donna went to Mexico for a week. I wasn't jealous cause it was Mexico not Costa Rica even though I don't know what Mexico is like for dogs. I think we all breathed a sigh of relief to see her let loose or whatever it is she does for relaxation. Funny thing was that our house sold while we were away. Yup, one week on the market and gone. Ma was pretty shocked when she came back, and the reality came fast. Possession date was June first. This was April.

With some reservation, she sent her letter of resignation to the ministry to find new homes for the kids in her home. I think it must have felt very unrealistic for Ma to do this as I so remember her saying that she cannot imagine her life without kids, so many times. Even her sister Auntie Patti said the stars were aligning here and this was good news. Felt like it. Deepak Chopra has said, "Life is meant to be lived in uncertainty." He has said he and his family lived in uncertainty for a year and they loved it. Here's the difference: Deepak has millions of dollars, my Ma does not!

But hey I can't help feeling stimulated to know we are going on another trip. Notice my vocabulary improving. woof

woof). A year in Mexico feels like a healing of mind, body, and spirit. I can tell you my ears are pointed up and my tail is a waggin, I seriously feel my body vibrating. This really sounds like fun. Even Ms Mugly, I mean Ms. Talula looks happier. She is doing her stupid dance, where she sits on her bum and moves all around the living room. Fool dog. Energy once again changing happy changes.

33

Towards the end of April I began packing up my home. It was a large, lovely home. All my foster kids were gone now, just me and the mutts. It was about this time I began having problems with my eyes. They ached, I even chose to watch TV with my eyes closed because it calmed the pain, yikes. I went to the Optometrist and had all the tests done. The good thing was nothing seemed to be wrong with my eyes. I was so happy about that as I was scared to death of going blind. I was also nervous because I had a new doctor because my old one retired, and here again is the dreaded word "change." This doctor would become another angel in my journey of life.

He ran a bunch of tests and, with no results of why my eyes were hurting. He stated that he tried to determine what this was and suggested a chest x-ray. I was amused, then I became agitated. I didn't want to do that, but did it anyways. Spent some time wondering why I was so agitated about this x-ray. Never did find an answer The doctor calmed me telling me no news is good news.

In May, Ma and Winnie decided to go to her home town for three days to spend with Gramma and family as this was the only time she had available before Mexico and she would be missing her gramma's eightieth birthday in late June. Ma felt so bad about that.

So, she and Winnie and Auntie Patti surprised Gramma and, boy, did they have a good time. Ma says it was one of the best trips home ever. She sure looked happy. They had surprised Gramma, and Ma says it was like a weekend girlfriend pyjama party. Winnie was a smash! She is a very likeable child. It was fun to show her all the homes Ma lived in, schools she went to, and share this with her.

34

When Ma got back, she had two messages from her doc's office saying they wanted her to come to the office. O' oh … Ma knew this couldn't be good news. So, off to the doc she went.

He explained to her that there was a shadow showing up on her lung and he wanted to do another chest x-ray. Ma wasn't worried cause this had happened once before. The doc explained if the shadow still existed, she would have to change her plans of going to Mexico and continue tests here for lung cancer. O' boy. Here is a word no one wants to hear.

When Ma got home she went on the internet. She says nowadays you can find information on absolutely everything. The trouble, she says, is one gets too much information and lots of times the wrong information that could scare the "you know what" out of you. Interesting enough, she read that one of the signs of lung cancer is sore eyes. Can you believe that? Ma says she didn't know if that was good news or bad news but was too busy now and had to concentrate on packing and downsizing a five-bedroom home before June first. Everything was going into storage except for me and Ms. Talula, thank the animal gods.

The closer it got to June the more anxious Ma was getting. I must admit, Ms. Talula and I were feeling anxiety as well. I'm afraid we were not acting at all like good kids. Snipping at each other, growling, as well as overwhelming Ma by not leaving her side. I think we were a little scared at this point. I also think we were feeling Ma's energy. Dogs have an amazing sense of energy you know. We can detect changes before humans can. Just ask my Ma. Thank the animal gods for a mom who understands and empathizes with us and takes the time to assure us all is OK. Lots of hugs and holding and walks.

This feeling wasn't like when we went to Costa Rica; this feeling was different, and I can't explain it, but it was a feeling I don't want to feel again. I think Ms. Talula and I were so scared that she would pack us up and put us into storage too. We were so relieved when we saw our suitcases. That kind of relief, you know, it's like you didn't even know you were that anxious till it was over, then you felt it. Weird. I also knew that Ms. Talula didn't know what travelling to another country was like, and I would have to help her make the transition. What I liked about this is that I had something to concentrate on instead of worrying. Make sense? Ma sure taught me well.

So, our flight for Mexico was for June 5. Ma found us what she called a funky apartment in Puerto Vallarta that took dogs. It was in this big old house, and she was excited. Not knowing Mexico, I trusted her judgment.

Ma says on the first of June, we had to move out of our home and into a motel for four days. Two sleeps later, Ma got news from her doc about that second chest x-ray. He told her the shadow was still there and a cat scan was needed.

Ma admitted she knew nothing about cat -scans, and the doc explained what this probably meant. First, he said the cat scan was an enlargement of a chest-x-ray and would show clearly where and how big this shadow was and that it really was a seeker of cancer. Yup, there's the word we are all avoiding. Ma says she went into la-la land.

"What the heck is la-la land?"

She said, "It is a place outside of your body. You are in your body, but you are not." *OK, forget I asked.*

She asked her doc what she should do as we were flying to Mexico in two days, and the doc suggested she put off Mexico and get the cat scan done immediately.

Ma thought about this for a few hours and recognized there was such little time to make a decision. She called the woman who rented her the apartment in Mexico and explained what happened. Her name was Mollie. Apparently, Mollie was familiar with all types of medical problems and had a lot of experience with doctors in Mexico, she said. Molly was probably near eighty-five years old. Trust her.

"Come on down, lots of good doctors here and have your cat scan here, no problem."

Ma made the decision; we would go to Mexico and see what happens. What Ma realized very quickly was now we were homeless, and options were not as easy as before. I cannot remember even what those days at the motel were like. Life seemed very unusual. It was like the three of us bonded closer than ever and looked out for each other. Ma made sure we got our food, treats, walks etc. She says she was so happy to have us to look after, that we were her saving grace in a world turned upside down. Huh? Nope not asking. And we love Uncle Al who was by Ma's side throughout all this drama.

Everybody needs a friend like that. I feel I have that in Ms. Talula now that I am over myself. I didn't even know till now how much I needed her in my life too. Wow, who would have thought? Ma, that's who.

On the morning we left for Mexico, Uncle Al came to drive us to the airport. It was all so emotional! He got us into the airport and after lots of hugs, he left us. Life as we knew it was over.

35

Well, here we are in Puerto Vallarta. The people, the noise … Lordy, lordy, this is going to be some adventure! Poor Ms. Talula looks like she's been run over by a truck. To be honest, I kinda feel the same way. We have this huge apartment above a restaurant. There are six dogs in this building and it is always noisy. The restaurant has a live band. Every day it plays the same Mexican music, all day, all evening. Ma seems to be fine with it, which gives us a measure of peace. Don't forget that dogs need continuity and that had been blown to hell. Sorry Ma! We even have our own pee room; this tickled my ma pink. She still takes us for our daily walks thank the animal gods.

Molly! What a personality. She is, like, really old, and delightful. She has her daughter Maria living with her, they live upstairs, and Maria has two schnauzers. They are really cute. Maria took one look at Ms. Talula and asked Ma if she could give her a haircut. Ma never wanted her to have one cause she believed Ms. Talula's hair color would lose that beautiful red shine. What shine ma? When she sees the photo of Ms. Talula back then she cracks up laughing. She was surprised she didn't notice how stupid Ms. Talula looked. Maria did a beautiful job. Even I appreciate the new look.

Ma went to see a doctor for her CT scan. Ma says when she met the doctor, she was surprised how young and good looking this man was. Trust Ma to go there. It was a little scary. She lay on a table like apparatus and with a hood over her head and a nurse came up to her, a very young nurse, and began to put a needle in Ma's hand. Ma says she freaked out a little. No one told her she would be getting a needle. The nurse simply said, "No Ingles!"

Ma says she closed her eyes, and said to God, "Well, God, it looks like it's you and me now for real." And gone was the anxiety.

News of the scan came back pretty fast. She needed a biopsy.

So, the doctor sent her to yet another specialist that does these biopsies. When Ma met this doctor, she saw that he was even younger than the other doctor and as handsome. Ma asked with a smile how old he was. He didn't answer. He did, however, invite her for a walk on the boardwalk! He also advised her to go home. He stated that although they had great doctor's in Puerto Rico, one has to go to Mexico for skilled anesthesiologists. It could mean the difference between life and death.

Ma came home and had some decisions to make. What stayed in her head was this: "Where is home?" Ma never did meet him on the boardwalk. LOL.

One day we dogs were on the patio when we saw something so awful, we barked and barked till Ma came running. In the tree protruding onto our patio were two frightening beings looking at Ms. Talula and me and, boy, *were we afraid. Ma, seeing what we were seeing ran into her apartment to get a camera. "Really, Ma." It was iguanas! Big iguanas. She laughed and laughed. We, on the other hand, or paw, did not find this so funny. What if they eat us? Ma assured us, that would not happen. I find we had to take a leap of faith here. Lordy, lordy.*

One day we were on a walk, going over a walking bridge that led to the boardwalk. There were two men ahead of us; they were probably thirty years of age. Ms. Talula accidentally bumped into one. The look that man gave Ma scared her far more than the iguanas. Ma realized this wasn't the safest place she could be at this time. She knew that it only takes one person to dislike you as a foreigner or race or whatever and as a single woman, it is even more important to be cautious. It was yet again a reminder that anything could happen at any time. So, she had to figure out where our home was.

36

I had to return to Canada but now realized I was very lonely. With no job, no home, and a biopsy needed, I felt overwhelmed.

I was having this profound journey that left me breathless. My world had turned upside down. I was at such a loss. God bless Maria. I overwhelmed her with my worries, and she was a saint. Yet, even she began to stay away from me. I know I was somewhat toxic. Lots of calls to my family and friends.

Winnie was now living in another town and begged me to come to her home, said she had a nice yard for the dogs, and she could look after me there. It was lovely to know that she was there for me.

My family wanted me to come home; my friends wanted me back on the Island and look at all my choices. Another angel in my corner was my little sister Patti whom I adore. We have each other's backs, and I knew she was feeling pretty powerless to help through this experience. She prays, a lot. Blessings Patti! Going from negative to the positive. Yes. I am going home. My home is the Island.

# # #

Our adventure in Mexico lasted only a few sleeps. We were supposed to stay much longer than that, you should see all the stuff Ma brought. Now it's all packed up again. Oy! On the day we were leaving, Ms. Talula and I were downright happy. I think this was the first time I saw Ms. Talula's tail wag. Have you seen her tail? It's not a tail; it is what I call a nub. And when it wags, it makes me laugh, although I was terrified Ma would leave without me. Believe me when I say I was watching her every move! When the taxi came to get us, Ma was taking Ms. Talula and her crate to the taxi first. Well, I freaked out. I knew my worst nightmare was coming true, and she was going to leave me in Mexico. The maid forgot to close the gate and off I went chasing Ma. Now, the streets in Mexico are not like the streets in Canada. One doesn't stop for people or dogs on the streets of Mexico. And traffic is non-stop. When Ma saw me running toward her, she nearly had a heart attack. Can you believe that not one car hit me? This was one busy street. She was kinda mad at me but too grateful to give me heck. She also instantly knew that the gods were looking after her and us! Ma calls it divine intervention.

And, yes, I had to ask Ma, "What is divine intervention?"

She said, "It means that the gods step up and intercept bad things happening and turns them into good things happening. And when this happens, it is always a surprise cause it doesn't happen a lot. So, once again, Zoey, gratitude! Don't ask the why, just say thank you!"

Ma first took us to Calgary to stay with Winnie who kinda lied about the yard. O' boy, Ma was agitated. Winnie couldn't decide which doggie beds to get, so she got them two each. We loved that! She knew that Winnie wanted to do all she could for Ma. Yet Ma knew that this wasn't where she needed to be. Ma told Winnie she had to go back to the Island. Winnie was terribly disappointed. Ma knew that betrayal of self is the highest betrayal. Ma needed to do what she felt was right for her.

After a few days we are at the airport again. Now, here we are at the Calgary airport and I have my doggie bag for inside the place with Ma, and Ms. Talula has her crate for storage on the plane when Ma was informed that there was a limit to the number of dogs on board, and it was full. She said Ma needed to put me in Ms. Talula's crate with Ms. Talula. Ma was seriously shaken. She put me and Ms. Talula together, and in seconds we were fighting.

You have to understand, at home we both have our own crates; they are our safe zones. Now you want one to intrude in another's crate? Uh uh. Ma almost cried. The nice lady saw what was happening and told Ma she would allow me to join Ma on the plane and did it for no charge. Gratitude was high on my list for West Jet that day. Big shout out to you West Jet. One never knows how a small kindness can so change a very bad day.

37

Landing on the Island felt like coming home! I was so happy to see my friend Big Al. I believed I was in the right place. All of a sudden, I had so much to do.

Took us a month to find an apartment that took dogs. It was cute apartment. The dogs seemed happy. *"Ma, as long as we are with you, we are always happy. It doesn't matter where we live. It does matter who we live with."*

"Oh my, Zoey, you are a gift!"

Now it's time for my biopsy. Here's the problem: they didn't give me enough freezing! I, for the life of me, cannot imagine what a foreign object was doing inside my body, the feel of it was so foreign to me that I went into hysterics. Which tells you a lot about this experience as I am not a histrionic person. All I could hear through my tears was "Oh no, we didn't give her enough freezing." I did get a heated sheet which they wrapped around my imagined abused body. The heated sheet was like having love surround me. I'm sure this sounds stupid, but in my limited vocabulary, this is the best description I have.

I was shivering and crying and felt I was back in my childhood abuse. It was one of the worst experiences in my life. A tip for others is if you are scared of needles, they can put you to sleep. I suggest you do.

Did I mention my real estate agent Diane was my caregiver that day? As a matter of fact for some strange reason, she took it upon herself to be my caregiver through the entire journey of this process as, in fact, it was proven I did indeed have lung cancer and needed to have one-third of my lung removed. Lots of medical appointments. Diane was there for all of it. Including being there during my surgery. Which is getting ahead of myself. I found that angels in my days came from the strangest of people. People I didn't expect to show up and be of service to me and as well, people who were not as kind. Fascinating.

I was told by my surgeon that I had to quit smoking now before the surgery or no surgery. Great! I needed my cigarettes. I had big anxiety! But I quit with attitude, I must admit. It is easy to go into victim mode when life hands you lemons. Easy to be all spiritual when life is going smoothly. I felt like my control was gone, my power was gone, and I realized I am going to have to find a new normal and quickly. For twenty-plus years, I have kept a gratitude journal (another Oprah tip). Every night before sleep, I write down five things that I am grateful for in my day. I sometimes asked myself what good does this do?

I believe that it puts your sleepy mind in a positive space instead of worrying about the crazies of the day. Sometimes it was time consuming to find five grateful things. But during this process, I was amazed to find I not only had five things of gratitude in my day, I could easily find five more. What I noticed is this: From morning to night, I seemed to be more alert, hypersensitive, paid attention to much more detail in people I saw in a day. It surprised me who stepped up to be there for me and also surprised at who did not. I hold no animosity, just an observation as they were so very clear, and it was exciting for me.

I asked my mother if she would fly down to take care of me and the dogs during surgery. She didn't hesitate. She was down so fast. God bless that woman. She became my rock, and nothing was off limits to her to help. And there was still Diane keeping us all together and supervising. I seemed to have high-highs and low-lows. Thank God the low-lows were fewer and did not last long.

One day, I was sitting in my room and just burst out crying. The message I kept going over in my head was "I can't do this." At this moment, my best friend Big Al walked into my room and simply told me, "Yes, you can." That simple acknowledgement went a long way in my journey here. I can and did. Big Al was someone I knew I could always count on. He is the definition of what a friend is. And gratitude to his wife for letting him share his friendship with me and not being jealous or worry about that.

It was during this part of my crazy journey that I came to the realization that I do not have many friends. I came to the realization that I have amazing friends.

My biggest support, believe it or not, came from my dogs. Zoey and Ms. Talula sensed something amiss and stayed very close to my side. They did not fight as often nor bark as often and gave me a reason every day to exercise and to have something besides my woes to concentrate on. Zoey and Ms. Talula received a gift from this experience. No more sleeps in their kennels. In bed with me. I so needed their snoring, bad breaths, their bodies nestled somewhere on my side. Talk about gratitude.

38

A week before my surgery, I had to have a mini surgery. They slit my throat and put a camera down to see that there were no lesions on my nymph nodes. Now this process was surprising. Because it was surgery, I was taken to the surgery room. Now in the hallway of that room is a row of patients on their beds waiting for their turn. I was so amused. I don't know why but I was. Then they gave me some type of anesthetic that sent me to the moon! It was glorious. Even though it lasted for only a moment or so. Someone told me it was propofol, Michael Jackson's choice of sleep aid. Propofol is a general anesthetic used to relax a patient before surgery. And boy was I relaxed. It was absolutely dreamy! And yes, this surgery was successful, no lesions on my lymph nodes. Major surgery was coming up.

On the morning of my surgery, I once again find myself in the row of bodies waiting for their surgery. I'm kind of excited to get that propofol again. But guess what, they didn't give me that anesthetic. I have no idea what they gave me but, boy, was I pissed. And they knew it. I went under with big attitude and anger because I didn't have my propofol! Now it is so darned funny. And embarrassing. Thank God my surgeon had a good sense of humor. My surgeon later tells me how comical it all was. Oh dear. I have an addictive personality, with no drugs or alcohol in over twenty-odd years, so having a legitimate drug was simply a gift for this alcoholic. Ha ha.

The following morning, a nurse came into my room and said, "Guess what, Rennie, you have 100% on something." I never remember on what, I was so excited to have 100% period. She asked what my secret was and without thinking, I said, gratitude. And it was true. I realized all those gratitude moments I wrote for twenty-five years led to this. I was humbled.

Now removed was one-third of my lung, and the healing took two months. I was just so happy to be home to see my mother and the mutts. They seemed pretty darned happy to see me. My mother had a problem keeping them off my bed, as she was worried about my stitches. Dogs seem to know there is a boo-boo, seriously. I can't describe this in adult terms. They become so gentle in their response to their sick ma. Zoey could not leave my side. Oh, the kisses. My lord. It was nice to be home.

My Mother stayed two weeks taking care of us all and even cooked my favorite, cabbage rolls and perogies, left in the freezer. Big, big gratitude. My mother has turned into an angel!

39

Now we wait. Question is for what? I was still waiting for this lawsuit to be over with so I could go back to fostering. In the meantime, I had to learn patience. I wondered then if I could think of anything else I could get into. I realized, no, I needed to be a foster parent. It was my happy place. I will wait.

Soon, I answered a knock on the door. A man asked if I was Rennie, I said yes, and he said, "You have been served." Served what? Yup, I am once again being sued. The nice lady and man who bought my house is suing me for rats, ants, and negligence.

If I tell you this rocked my world, it would be an understatement. Now I have two lawsuits?

I decided to go see them and ask them why. They told me they couldn't talk to me, that I had to talk to their lawyer. Then she talked, a lot. They were revamping our home. I loved that house. On the island it is said, who doesn't have rats? We were so surrounded by nature. I clearly let this woman know that we had rats. I had even showed her where the rat traps were.

I had let her stay in my home before the possession date and explore the house. She had never mentioned rats. The day before I left for Mexico, I stopped in, and she declared, "Rennie, it's not rats, it's squirrels", she saw them running around.

"No," I said, "it's rats."

"No," she said, "it's squirrels."

"OK then, its squirrels." At this point we were almost friends. That changed drastically.

She told me I hired bad people to do my carpentry work and that's how she got the negligence factor. About three months after that, I got another knock on my door, same guy as before.

"Are you Rennie?"

"Yes," I said.

"You have been served." What?

Here's the thing: When this nice lady sued me, she also sued her building inspector. When you're the property buyer, you hire an inspection company to visit the home in question. The company inspects it from top to bottom, then writes a final analysis that tells the buyers the good and bad of the house. Buyers then have a choice to buy or not to buy. It is a protection for home buyers. Believe this or not, the buyers did not share my questionnaire report with the building inspector.

When this building inspector got served, he decided, he wasn't at fault at all, this is Rennie's fault and sued me. It had been eight months since I had quit smoking. This last lawsuit put me on my knees, and I spoke with God, "God, not one, not two, but three lawsuits and lung cancer." I lit up. Been smoking ever since.

158

I remember the deposition. The nice lady had a woman lawyer. Whew! She was very aggressive, and I do mean aggressive. At one point she asked me if I knew a certain name. I said, "No, never heard of him."

She said, "It's your neighbour." I began to laugh. I only have two neighbours. One is friendly and the other is not. She was talking about the one who was not. I explained this to her. She said, "Would you be surprised that he told us that he told you he saw about one hundred rats on your property line?"

I answered, "Rats know where the property line is?" They don't like jokes in depositions. My lawyer kicked me under the table. I was so humored. Still am. It was so ridiculous I couldn't help myself. Another thing to know about me is the more nervous I become, the funnier I become. It just happens, and I have to work hard to control this in many cases.

I once again went to this nice lady and said, "Please drop your lawsuit on me." Her response was this: "In order to sue our building inspector, we had to sue you. Period."

I often think about this and remember a quote I once heard, "What you cause another person to experience, you will one day experience." I now knew she was going to go through with it. My hands were tied. There is another saying, if someone tells you about themselves, believe them. There were red flags, I didn't pay attention. As the kids say, my bad. This experience was far worse than what I have written.

This lawsuit settled two years later. About a year after this, I received a letter from my old address. I got so excited, I thought, maybe it's an apology! Not quite. She was simply mean. She had even suggested that my cancer was not from smoking but from mold. This, of course, is nonsense. Instead of writing back and letting her know what I thought about her, I chose to pray for her. It wasn't the first time someone has hurt me unnecessarily. AA taught me what you cannot control, let go. I prayed for her a lot.

Another life lesson I learned along the way is if you don't like someone, and have been hurt by them, instead of getting revenge, pray for them! Seriously? When I first heard this, I thought it was the stupidest idea I had ever heard. A lady once shared her example about this, she said that a co-worker of hers was very hard on her and was mean to her every day. She said going to work was getting very stressful. She was so tired of this. She decided she had nothing to lose and began to pray to God, "God," she said, "bless this bitch." And she said this every day for a long time. She began to notice something: the not-nice lady was still abusive to her, yet it didn't seem to bother her anymore. Something had changed, and because she no longer reacted to this not-nice lady, the insults became less and less till they were no more. It works. As well, during her prayer process, she found herself omitting the word bitch. I love this example! When I truly think about this process, it makes sense to me. If you pray for someone who is not very nice, the power of the prayer affects not only the mean person but also you. If the mean person suddenly has a spiritual change, look at how wonderful it is for her and for future victims. Somehow, instead of being a victim to them, you become not only a survivor of them, your prayers become their gift and they don't even know it. I love it.

40

After this lawsuit was settled, my lawsuit from the building inspector was dropped and guess what? My lawsuit from the ministry was settled as well. I was so happy.

I called the ministry to talk about a new contract for fostering. It was time to go house hunting, settle down, get back to my children. I was so excited.

Nope, not happening. I was told from the higher-ups in the ministry who have never met me that they believed I was a danger to the next child moving in. What? That was literally said to me. And I was blindsided.

God bless Xanax. This answer went straight to my heart. Anxiety became full blown. They never let me go, I resigned, knowing I would be back in a year to a smaller home and foster two children, not four. There was no animosity after my exit. And now, not only did they not want me, they didn't want me anywhere in BC.

I would call different towns that were thrilled with my resume till they called my ministry for reference and I would get a call back saying there was no financing for my contract. Which was such a bold lie. Everyone knows the ministry is always looking for foster parents, especially with the wealth of experience I had.

This experience was so much worse for me than the cancer experience. In the next two years I wondered what to do with my life. I felt so lost. Not knowing what my future held was messing up my spirituality. I was forgetting all my wonderful tools I had learned in the past twenty-five years. I remember thinking, it's easy to be all spiritual when life is going well. How spiritual are you when life bites? Once again, I am forever grateful to AA and my family there; they kept me grounded and their support got me through with all the love they had.

And I continued to show gratitude every night. You would think that with all this going on, gratitude would be hard to come by. Wrong. Amazingly enough, every day that I struggled, I had taught myself to look for the good in even a bad day. This profoundly lightened my load, thus remembering that not all was wrong with my days.

A year after I took a trip off Island to the Okanagan, I had a meeting with a ministry in their neck of the woods. I explained everything to them. They said, "Let's wait and see." That wait took a year, when one day I got a phone call from the Okanagan. "Rennie, we have a contract for you." I cried!

Looks like I had to leave the Island, but life is just an adventure anyways. Funny thing. Just before I left for the Okanagan, for some reason I was talking with these higher-ups once again, and I cannot remember why. What I do remember is them telling me if I did well in the Okanagan, they would consider taking me back. Really? Prayers for the higher-ups! My frustration with the higher-ups is this, they have no idea who I am as a person or a worker. They have never met me or seen me. There needs to be a different process in how foster parents are treated.

I would have preferred to have been asked to sit in front of a board of some sort and plead my case. Especially being in the business of caring. I hear so many stories about people thrown under the bus in so many walks of life after twenty to thirty-plus years of service. Not just by the ministry. I think everyone knows someone who has been hurt like me.

For me, it was important to not go into victim mode yet again. It certainly took me awhile, and I'm sure I have PTSD but guess what, I didn't drink or do drugs, didn't attempt suicide. This tells me how much I have grown in my journey. I was also so grateful that I did not have to leave BC. I love BC. "My mutts, we are off to the Okanagan on another adventure!" I am empowered once again!

41

Before I left for the Okanagan, I decided to go to Mexico once again for three weeks. I wanted to see Molly and her daughter again. I also decided this time round to take Ms. Talula as it was her turn to travel with me. I wished I could have taken both of them. Ms. Talula deserved some Ma time for once.

I took Zoey to Uncle Al's for the duration and felt so guilty! She loves Uncle Al. She hates being left without me. I can't say I blame her. Think about how this process goes. I take them both to see Uncle Al and then run out the door with Ms. Talula, leaving Zoey stunned.

I think it's mean. I'm sure Zoey experienced anxiety, thanx to me.

"Hey Ma, it was mean! You blind- sided me!"

While Zoey was miserable, Ms. Talula and I were having a blast. It is so much more relaxing with one dog than two. And Zoey, every day I felt guilty thinking of you.

I was in Mexico for a week when my little sister Patti spontaneously decides to come down for a week. What fun. My favorite time with her was going for a long walk in the early evening, up roads, down roads, left and right, and we got lost. Patti kept telling me to stop talking with strangers in this Mexican barrio. Which just makes me talk to more of them! We began to walk up a mountain and by now it was getting dark, and fast. We even had a dog posse running after Ms. Talula. Patti picked up Ms. Talula so fast, and we ran. It was one of those adventures that still has me smiling. Patti was worried because we were lost, no cabs around, no restaurants, the darkness. When all of a sudden, we see a light outside the barrio! And traffic! Soon after we found a cab and home we went. I have never had so much fun being lost. I think Patti loved it too.

One day we were walking to a Starbucks, and I was window shopping, and Patti called out, "Come on, Rennie, I need my coffee!" I hurried up to her.

I yelled out, "Coffee!" and there was this guy who looked at Patti and asked, *"Tu nombre es Coffee?"* (Your name is Coffee?).

Patti said, *"Si, senior,"* and this name has stuck ever since. Coffee loves it.

Another day I was downtown with Ms. Talula when this young teenage girl asked me what Ms. Talula's name was, so I told her, and she looked angry and said, "She's a girl, why you call 'her' Mr. Lula?"

I laughed so hard, saying, "No, it's Ms. Talula, not Mr. Lula." She got quite the laugh as well. I think Ms. Talula had a wonderful time.

I did manage to get down to see Molly and she was so happy to see that I was alive. Aww. Marie was not around, so it was a short visit. I was happy to see Molly at least.

At home, the first thing I did was run to Big Al's to get Zoey. I could tell she was happy to see me but pretty mad that I had left her in the first place. Her tail was a wagging, but she seemed stand-offish. Not her usual self. *"Really, Ma, you feel that? You feel my confusion? At the same time, I missed you and that monkey dog so, so much."*

She and Ms. Talula slept with me that night, and the next morning I noticed this awful smell, till I realized it smelled like poop. Poop? What the heck! I looked around and could smell it, just couldn't see it. My bedspread is a lovely brown with coral flowers. I soon found the poop! This was Zoey's revenge! She has never done this before. I could almost see the gleam in her eyes. I seriously think she grinned at me. I could not stop laughing once again. Seems like after that, Zoey got over her hurt.

"That's right! I did it," said Zoey. "I was so mad that you had the cajones to go away without me (and I don't even know what cajones are), not only without me but you took "that" dog with you. I thought I was your travelling dog. I know it wasn't a very nice thing to do and I felt kinda bad. OK then, no, I didn't."

I reminded Zoey that, in the past, she was the one I took on many trips, leaving Jazzie, and he handled this far better than she did. She seemed to think about what I said, giving me kisses.

"I hear you, Ma, but here's the thing, I am not Jazzie!"

42

The Okanagan, wow, I like this place. We have a really funky house here. Guess what, we even have a doggy door. Holy, who invented these things? Never mind bells, all Ms. Talula and I had to do when we wanted to go out was go through our own door. Can you imagine? What fun. They even have this very nice beach and we walk there a lot. Here is what I learned through this part of my journey, it doesn't matter where I live, home to me is where the heart is. As long as I'm with my ma, life is good. And, too, watching my Ma return to her old self, happy! She has again a garden to reorganize, a home to decorate, children's bedrooms to prepare. If Ma had a tail, it would be wagging!

I believe that it was around this time I began to feel very tired. I even found it difficult to wag my tail. It all takes a strength I no longer have. What my ma noticed was I no longer wanted to walk. She assumed it was cause I was spoiled, and I couldn't blame her for that. After all the times I stubbornly refused to move. Yet she didn't hold this against me and instead you know what she bought me a stroller. That's right. You read right! I was so impressed. I loved this thing. I once again felt very royal! She said I have earned the right to be more spoiled as I was now in my seventies. This went on for about two months.

What Ma doesn't know is I am going blind. I know, sad, right? The reason Ma doesn't know this shows you how good I was at knowing exactly where everything in my home is. I do today, what I did yesterday, in the same places, which is one of the gifts of continuity for dogs. The most important sense I have right now is knowing where my ma's lap is. My eyesight may be going, yet my kisses are strong. And I seem to be doin a lot of lickin these days. If I am not in my favorite bed sleeping, I am spending a lot of time lying on Ma's stomach. I love this feeling; it is like nesting. I was even enjoying Ms. Talula. I

I realized Zoey was slowing down. I kept a watch on her every day, noticing her need to sleep a lot more. She has her favorite bed and between eating and peeing, you could find her there or lying on my stomach. She seemed to need to be near me all the time. I watched carefully to see if she was experiencing any pain. She did not appear to be. I truly believed she was simply experiencing old age.

The final day played out like this: it was morning and the dogs were on my bed when I wakened. Ms. Talula jumped down to follow me and as I watched, my darling Zoey walked right off the bed onto the floor. This was the first time I realized she was blind. My heart hurt.

It was then I knew the end was here. I held her so tight and cried and cried. Her body was as light as a feather. She cuddled into my neck, barely moving. I could not believe that Zoey's time was up. We spent all of this last day together, I held her till it was time to take her to her animal doc. The doc too, realized Zoey's time was up. He told me Zoey was dying from old age. I held her close and talked to her while the final process took place.

"Zoey, may the sun shine upon you, may the love shine through you, and until we meet again, may God hold you in the palm of his hand."

As awful as it is, as beautiful as it is, it was peaceful. I felt her take her last breath and knew she was now entering the hereafter! I told her I would see her at the pearly gates and to wait for me. I also told her to look for Jazzie and Promise, that they would be waiting for her.

"Oh my God, Ma … guess who met me at the pearly gates? Jazzie, Promise, Mugs Malone, Hannah, and some cute little guy named Riley! We are all running around this beautiful field, no fear from any of the dogs here, and guess what, Ma? Lots and lots of monkeys! Ha! I laughed so hard, I peed right there. These ones are so charming. I can't wait for you to meet them. There are also dogs here who I don't know but they know you! There's Moochie, Muffin, Kiwi, and they all send their love.

"There's a lake that's not deep, blue as blue can be. There is absolutely no fear here, Ma, and there are trees with, are you ready? Cookies! They are called Cookie Trees. Holy moly, Ma! And they are so good. Fields and fields of green, flowers of every color. Speaking of flowers Ma, tell Ms. Talula there are fields of her favorite flowers here, dandelions! And the sky Ma, a brilliant blue. To be able to see color in all it's brilliance is so divine, it's pawsitively awesome!

"I'm not even tired; as a matter of fact, I feel fabulous. There are a lot of Rennie stories here, Ma … so, yes, lots of humor, doggie humor that is, and lots of love.

We are all waiting for you but take your time. We ain't going anywhere. Look for me, Ma, I am always there with you. And Ma, thank you for everything. I could not have asked for a better life. Please give my Ms. Talula a big hug from me and let her know that I always did love her, even if I did have to share her."

I know my Zoey is now in doggie heaven, running around, having fun. I also know she doesn't have to miss me; she is beside me always.

And with knowing all this, my heart still aches for this girl. She truly was a special friend. And I am so very grateful to have shared eleven wonderful years with a mutt who knew how to put a smile on my face every day.

"Zoey, I am looking forward to seeing you in front of the pearly gates. Don't be late! Love, Ma."

43

I once heard this scenario: "look at every soul you meet knowing that every one of them is "enlightened". The only one "not" enlightened is you! This teaches us that every soul put in your path is there to teach you something about yourself!

I have read so much spiritual material in my journeys and have met amazing angels crossing my path. Here is some of the best advice I got at the beginning of this journey: "You will read or hear a lot of ideas, opinions, advice. Some, you will agree with, others you will not. Take what you like and leave what doesn't fit your ideals."

Here is a belief that I can share with you. I, of course, believe in reincarnation. I believe we have lived many, many lives and will continue till I reach some sort of "nirvana" that I am not even close to. Let me depict a scenario for you to understand my belief in the hereafter.

Imagine yourself sitting on a cloud with your spirit angels who have been with you for eons. You are talking about moving on to your next life. In this conversation, you and your angels discuss what you have learned in past lives, including this one, of course, your strengths and weaknesses. Now the conversation changes to what lessons you need to learn in your future life, to strengthen those leftover weaknesses.

Here's my scenario: On my last hereafter, I was once again on that cloud with my angels and we chose for this life, my mother, for exactly who she was, with all her warts and wisdoms, then my dad for exactly who he was, and all my sisters for exactly for who they were, and then my husband, and best friends etc…

They were the main people who in this life was going to give me the opportunities to grow in areas I need to attend to in this life. When I look back at my life, I realize some of my successes have been overcoming being a victim of incest, alcoholism, surviving cancer and, yes, I am ten years cancer-free at this writing. And from these came growth after growth after growth. Kind of like having had the glass half empty kind of life, to having the glass half full. It has been an extraordinary journey and it's not over yet.

Turning my foster home experience into a fostering career has been the biggest reward to have chosen. There are over 250 children who have crossed my path, lived in my home, shared my journey. Sharing their journey has been a privilege and an honour. I pray it was a job well done. Big blessings to each child and thank you.

The one conversation I will be having with God in the hereafter is old age. I feel that for all of us experiencing old age is like a smack in the face! We get through all life's ups and downs and there were so many ups and downs that we should all be showered with gifts of love and care in our declining years.

And people say, "Now we are in the golden years."

"What golden years?" It seems to me that in today's society, in North America at least, elders are not treated nearly as well as in the past. What I see is not comforting to me as I get older. I'm sure this is the final area of my life for more opportunities to have faith in God and to keep my glass half full to the end! I pray I move forward with grace!

And lastly, to every dog, cat, bird, racoon, deer, that have graced my home, thank you from the bottom of my heart. My home would be merely a house if you were not there to share it with me. The daily gifts of laughter from each of my animals has made each of my days that much more sunnier. I cannot imagine a life without animals. The lessons they have taught me has mostly been "unconditional love".

For that alone, I am eternally grateful!

The End!

Acknowledgements

This author wishes to acknowledge the following:

My Ma for always being available to listen to the next chapter, time and time again. Her unconditional love consistently present. Always my cheer leader, prompting me forward.

Katie Heinrichs, my very own personal editor who offered sage advice, criticism, life time friendship, and much love.

For Winnie, my one and only daughter, who insisted I become her "mom". You have given me a window of opportunity to know what having my own child feels like. You do not disappoint. Thank you for my granddaughters Amina (Baby Pineapple, Aliya (Baby Carrot) and for my new name, (Grandma Tomato). You have been a shining light in a sometimes very dark period of time. Thank you.

A.A. for being my foundation in a life of sobriety. If it was not for this family of love, I cannot imagine what my future would have held. For every member, regardless of time spent in the rooms, "keep coming back" and thank you for being you.

For all my past foster parents. I use this opportunity to thank every one of you who took me into your homes. As a long time foster parent myself, I have immense respect and appreciation for the foster homes who opened their doors to me, in my time of need.

To every child who has walked through my doors and shared my home. Each one of you has taught me something about myself and for that I am grateful. Through the good and bad, the ups and downs, you each have touched my heart. I pray always for you, peace and joy in your life.

Gezel Zozobrado, my project manager at Tellwell Publishing. Thank you for your patience, and guidance and for not giving up on me. I know how frustrating I can be and your kindness shone through.

Rachel Peterson, my editor at Tellwell Publishing. Job well done Rachel. Thank you for your kind words, your wisdom, your editing.

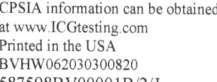

CPSIA information can be obtained
at www.ICGtesting.com
Printed in the USA
BVHW06203030300820
587598BV00001B/2/J

9 780228 822776